A YEAR OF
LIVING KINDFULLY

A YEAR OF LIVING KINDFULLY

Week-by-week activities that will enrich your life through

SELF-CARE and KINDNESS TO OTHERS

ANNA BLACK

CICO BOOKS
LONDON NEW YORK

Published in 2020 by CICO Books
An imprint of Ryland Peters & Small Ltd
20–21 Jockey's Fields,   341 E 116th St,
London WC1R 4BW   New York, NY 10029

www.rylandpeters.com

10 9 8 7 6 5 4 3 2 1

A CIP catalog record for this book is available
from the Library of Congress and the British
Library.

ISBN: 978-1-78249-820-9

Printed in China

Editor: Dawn Bates
Designer: Eliana Holder
Illustrator: Amy-Louise Evans
Art director: Sally Powell
Production manager: Gordana Simakovic
Publishing manager: Penny Craig
Publisher: Cindy Richards

CONTENTS

MINDFULNESS + KINDNESS
= KINDFULNESS

INTRODUCTION

How would it feel to spend the next year being kinder and more compassionate—to learn to live your life with more heart? The practices and weekly activities in this book encourage you to explore cultivating both kindness and compassion for yourself, others, and the world you live in.

Becoming kinder and more compassionate is a process, and not something that will happen overnight. In much the same way we might cultivate a garden by planting seeds, tending them as they germinate and grow, creating space by removing weeds, and nourishing growing shoots with water, sunlight, and other essentials, it is about the long game. There are times when our garden may be a bit neglected or when it feels as if nothing is happening, but as long as we don't give up and continue to give it attention some of the seeds we have planted will flourish. The practices in this book require the same attitude, but instead we are cultivating intention and learning to be more kindful of our thoughts and behavior.

MINDFULNESS

There is a long-standing history of cultivating compassion and kindness within Buddhism with the Loving Kindness practices, as well as through mindfulness. Kindness is implicit in the practice of the latter—the way we pay attention to our experience is crucial. Mindfulness has been practiced for thousands of years, but the program that founded the secular modern mindfulness was developed by Jon Kabat-Zinn and his co-workers in the 1970s. More recently, the Mindful Self-Compassion (MSC) program developed by Christopher K Germer PhD and Kristin Neff PhD, and Mindfulness-based Compassionate Living (MBCL) by Erik van den Brink and Frits Koster, have combined mindfulness and compassion practices to build emotional resilience for a happier, healthier life. Van den Brink and Koster describe mindfulness and compassion as two sides of the same coin:

mindfulness allows us to see more clearly and gain insight into our experience, and compassion gives us a way of relating to any challenges that arise, so we don't become overwhelmed and are able to be with them safely.

While writing this book, I discovered that I was being more intentional about practicing kindness simply because it was at the forefront of my mind. I noticed that when I'm rushing I don't have the mental space to think about being compassionate or, if I do, I quickly dismiss it as "I don't have time." Yet when I give myself compassion and offer kindness to others, my life expands to make room and it feels richer for it. My kindness practice is always a work-in-progress and that's okay—every time I can be kinder to myself, others, or the world around me is a bonus. I hope the suggestions in this book show you how you can live a life interwoven with kindness, rather than it being another thing to do. One practice I particularly love because of its simplicity is this: I pause in the busyness of my day and ask myself, "What do I need right now?"

HOW TO USE THIS BOOK

In the first section you will discover how practicing kindness and compassion benefits others, how it is essential to your well-being, how to do it, and how to overcome those things that might get in the way. The practices and activities that follow give you the opportunity to tease apart the different layers of your experience, discovering how much you currently live a "kindful" life (or not), and suggest opportunities for intentionally cultivating kinder and more compassionate habits. You can do this as you go about your daily life—the informal practices that form the bulk of the weekly activities—as well as in a more formal way by meditating (see page 36).

It takes time to establish new habits—and let go of those that no longer serve. In the week-by-week section there are 52 opportunities over 12 months to explore ways you can live more kindfully. Intentionally focusing on kindness and compassion regularly over an extended period of time will help establish them as something you do naturally. There are some suggestions for how to support your ongoing practice on page 24 and supporting resources on page 188. Of course there

are going to be periods when you forget or life gets in the way—and whether you respond to yourself on those occasions with kindness or self-criticism is always another opportunity for practice.

My invitation to you is make an intention to show up to your life for the next 12 months. Make your daily life with all its trials, tribulations, successes, and triumphs— the large and the small—your practice. Make an intention to be kind—to others and to yourself.

REFLECTING

There are many proven benefits to cultivating kindness and compassion (see page 15), but as you work through this book, I'd encourage you to notice how practicing kindness and compassion affects *you* in terms of your mood and well-being.

Approach it as an experiment, with an open mind and without any preconceptions or expectations about what you will achieve or what is going to happen. To support you in this, there are reflection pages throughout the activities section and at the end of the book. Reflect, and record what you notice objectively. There is an opportunity to do a review halfway through the year as well as at the end, when you can look at the experiment as a whole, pull together insights and learning, and decide which kindness and compassion activities and practices are most helpful for you.

KINDNESS AND COMPASSION

Kindness is generally defined as the quality of being friendly, generous, and considerate. We most commonly think of kindness in relation to others, but how about being kind to yourself or the world you live in—within your neighborhood or the planet itself? What does kindness look like to you in these three domains?

Take a moment to reflect on the last few days—can you think of an occasion when you were kind to someone else? How about to the environment? And have you been kind to yourself? Is there one domain you find easier or harder than another?

We usually find it relatively easy to be kind to others, but we often struggle with being kind and compassionate to ourselves and, while there are reasons for that (see page 21), being kind to yourself is an antidote to self-criticism and self-judgment, both of which impact negatively on your mental well-being.

OTHERS: Being kind to others includes family, friends, neighbors, co-workers, and strangers. How does your willingness to offer kindness to a family member or friend differ from offering it to someone you don't know? When we are not emotionally invested in someone there can be a reluctance to take the time to do something different because there is no apparent payback. But is that true? How does it make you feel when you do something kind for someone else, whether you are personally connected or not?

SELF: We can practice kindness or its opposite—meanness—to ourselves in our **thoughts** (self-critical); **physically** toward our body—how we take care of it (or not), and what we put in it in the way of food and drink; **emotionally**—acknowledging and prioritizing what we need, exploring what drains or depletes us with a view of taking care of ourselves. In the first instance, practicing self-kindness often means letting go of practicing meanness toward yourself.

ENVIRONMENT: This simply means **the world around you**; it might be right outside your door, farther afield, or even the planet as a whole. Noticing whether you conserve or squander the earth's resources; cherish, neglect, or even harm the land, sea, and all that lives within—plants, trees, insects, birds, animals, fish, and so on.

Living kindfully encourages us to see how we are all interconnected and how we relate to each other and how our actions have an impact. What that impact is, is up to you.

COMPASSION

While kindness is the quality of being friendly, generous, and considerate, compassion is the quality of warmth, tenderness, sympathy, and empathy. When we feel compassion for someone, first we notice they are suffering and experience a "tug at the heart"—there's a sense of connection or understanding, an acknowledgment that the other person is in pain; this is combined with a desire to help or alleviate their suffering.

We can empathize with them and imagine ourselves in their shoes, rather than seeing ourselves as separate. Experiencing compassion for another includes a sense that we are all cut from the same cloth—we are all part of a common humanity.

We can offer compassion to ourself as well as others. Neff (see page 7) identifies three components of self-compassion and each has a polar opposite:

SELF-KINDNESS VERSUS SELF-JUDGMENT/SELF-CRITICISM

Self-compassion is when we treat ourselves the way we would treat another who is hurting, or who has made a mistake or let themselves down, rather than blaming and judging ourselves harshly.

COMMON HUMANITY VERSUS ISOLATION

When things go wrong or not as we hope there can be tendency to see it as all our fault—"I must have done something wrong." However, when practicing self-compassion we acknowledge that suffering, loss, and making mistakes are part of being human and we are all a work-in-progress; imperfect beings just doing the best we can, acknowledging lessons learned, and how we can do better next time.

Practicing self-compassion widens our perspective to acknowledge that whatever challenges we are experiencing, there will always be another individual somewhere who is experiencing something similar. We are also products of genetics, environment, upbringing—a mix of influences/factors that are outside of our control, but which have shaped us into the person we are. Instead of blaming ourselves for the parts we don't like or can't control, we can hold them tenderly (it's not our fault). We can learn to relate to ourselves differently—and cultivate more positive attitudes toward ourselves and take responsibility for making changes if we wish to.

MINDFULNESS VERSUS OVERIDENTIFICATION

Mindfulness helps us notice and acknowledge that we are suffering and gives us the clarity to see things as they are without adding unnecessary drama on top. It helps widen our perspective so we get a sense of the bigger picture, including our own role in whatever is unfolding. Without this clarity, we can get lost in over-thinking.

Self-criticism, isolation, and overidentification have been identified as the body's reaction to an internal threat (see page 19), so by addressing these by specifically practicing self-compassion is a way of activating the soothing response (see page 20), which turns off the body's stress reaction.

MINDFULNESS AND ITS ROLE

In order to discover what serves us—or not—first we have to become aware of it. This is where practicing mindfulness can help. Mindfulness is a trait that we can cultivate and strengthen. It is commonly defined as intentionally paying attention to our experience as it arises, without judging it or with kindly awareness.

By tuning into our experience, we see it more clearly. Mindfulness teaches us to become aware of our inner landscape—head (thoughts), heart (emotions), and body (physical sensations)—together with what is arising in the world around us; as well as the bare experience we also notice **how we are relating to it**—whether that is liking (wanting more), disliking (resisting it, wanting things to be different/go away), or being neutral (indifferent which may mean we tune out).

How we pay attention to our experience is essential, particularly when our experience is difficult—instead of judging it, we notice it with kindness, open-heartedness, gentleness, curiosity. This is an essential step in turning toward those parts of our experience that we instinctively resist and want to be different. It is this resistance that causes us so much unhappiness and it is only when we stop resisting and instead truly accept whatever is arising that our experience is transformed. We can't change our experience, but we can choose how we relate to it.

Mindfulness teaches us to see how things as they really are—rather than how we wish them to be.

TRAINING THE BRAIN

Scientists are discovering that the brain is more plastic than historically thought and that we can train it in the same way as we can train the body. Whether we being more attentive with mindfulness or cultivating qualities such as compassion and empathy, the more frequently we do it, the stronger those specific neural pathways in the brain become—just like a muscle being exercised. Likewise, "use it or lose it" applies—if we do nothing, those neural pathways wither and die. The activities and practices in this book will give you a compassion workout throughout the year; exercising those muscles of kindness, compassion, caring, connection, and empathy toward you, others, and the world you live in.

It is important to note that practicing compassion and/or mindfulness is not going to magically make your problems disappear. It is about cultivating a way to care and support yourself and others when suffering or facing difficulties—whether large or small—rather than curing or solving a problem.

THE BENEFITS OF CULTIVATING KINDNESS AND COMPASSION

Although the research into mindfulness and compassion is relatively new and continually evolving, there is much that is encouraging.

MINDFULNESS

There is an established body of evidence that mindfulness helps people cope more effectively with stress and be more accepting of whatever situation they find themselves in. People report feeling kinder to themselves and others, calmer, and having increased life satisfaction and decreased ill health. Rather than fixing a particular problem, practicing mindfulness changes our relationship to our experience, particularly the negative, helping us see patterns of behavior, think more clearly, and teaching us to pause before responding.

Self-reported benefits are supported by before and after brain scans of participants of an 8-week mindfulness course, which show increased activity in the areas of the brain related to compassion and empathy, as well as perspective-taking, focus, concentration, and attention, and a decrease in activity of the amygdala, the area of the brain which activates the body's stress reaction.

SELF-COMPASSION

Research into compassion has shown the following benefits for people who are self-compassionate:

- Better able to cope with life's ups and downs
- More willing to acknowledge and learn from mistakes and try again
- Make healthier lifestyle choices
- More understanding and accepting of personal imperfections, including aspects of character which may be down to genetics, environment, or upbringing, and thus out of their control

- Score highly on scales measuring wisdom, personal initiative, happiness, optimism, positive affect, and coping
- More sensitive to another's suffering, but able to regulate their own emotions so they can respond rather than walk away because it feels too painful.

Self-compassion is also related to life satisfaction, emotional intelligence, and connectedness. Higher levels of self-compassion relate to reduced self-criticism, perfectionism, anxiety, depression, and rumination (Germer, 2009).

When we are self-critical we are motivated by a fear of failure and disapproval, rather than curiosity and interest. This means when things don't go according to plan, we are more likely to give up rather than risk failing again. Self-criticism is more likely to lead us into unhelpful cycles of rumination, which switch on a negative view of ourselves and is a key driver for anxiety and depression.

LOVING KINDNESS

Loving Kindness is a traditional Buddhist practice to cultivate connection and kinship with yourself and others—both known and unknown. Neuro-imaging research shows that Loving Kindness practice transforms the area of the brain that deals with motivation. (See the Cultivating Kindness practice on page 63.)

MOTIVATION DRIVES INTENTION

INTENTION IS WHAT LIES BEHIND EVERY ACTION

Research into happiness has shown that although we may experience a spike in happiness when something happens like winning the lottery, we then settle surprisingly quickly back to our own baseline. This may suggest that all attempts to improve happiness are doomed, but a randomized control trial (Frederickson, Cohn, Coffey, Pek & Finkel, 2008) showed that one hour of Loving Kindness practice a week led to an increase over time of daily expressions of Loving Kindness which in turn led to an increase in a range of personal resources (such as mindfulness, purpose in life, social support, decreased ill health). This in turn led to increased life satisfaction and decreased depressive symptoms, together with enhanced positive emotions particularly when interacting with others. As the research found, Loving Kindness seems to be one positive emotion that continues long after the period of doing it in the meditation practice, i.e. we experience the benefits in everyday life, rather than in the meditation itself.

Loving Kindness practices also make us feel more socially connected—that is, more helpful, compassionate, empathetic, and less biased toward others, at a time when many societal changes are creating increased feelings of alienation and distrust.

REGULATING THE EMOTIONS

It's particularly important to find ways to be kind to ourselves when we are under a lot of stress and here is why.

The body has three emotion regulation systems: Threat, Drive, and Soothing. We are continually moving between these different states and all three are essential to our physical and emotional well-being.

THREAT: activated when the body faces danger (what we don't want), characterized by negative emotions (fear, aversion, anger). Threat is all about survival in the moment.

DRIVE: focuses on getting the resources we need to survive in the longer term: food, shelter, sexual partners, possessions, power (what we want). Drive's emotions are excitement, pleasure, arousal—pleasant but often fleeting and when we are thwarted at getting what we want or we lose it, these emotions can quickly become negative.

SOOTHING: is about calm, connection, bonding with others. Once all basic needs have been fulfilled we have the luxury of expanding our awareness. The emotions connected with "soothing" such as contentment, feeling safe and secure, and connected are more long-lasting than the pleasure emotions of Drive. The body releases endorphins and oxytocin (the so-called "cuddle" hormone) that give us a warm feeling in the heart when we strengthen connections with others.

THREAT

When we perceive something as a threat, the body's stress response is activated by the amygdala, which is located in the most primitive part of the brain. The body goes on alert and moves into battle-station mode in preparation for **fight** (attack the threat), **flight** (run away), or **freeze** (play dead). In the meantime, the body continues to gather

data on the perceived threat, including accessing memory. Based on this information, the alert will either be switched off or maintained so the way we think will influence this and negative thinking can keep us stuck in 'threat' mode. The more frequently the amygdala is activated, the more hypersensitive it becomes.

The stress response can be activated regardless of whether a threat is physical or psychological. Germer (see page 7) states that when the threat is internal, i.e. mental or emotional, and there is no physical enemy to fight, we turn in on ourselves instead. **Fight becomes self-criticism, flight becomes self-isolation,** and **freeze becomes self-absorption** or stuck in thinking. Neff's three components of self-compassion (see page 12) provide the antidote for each of these: self-kindness is the antidote for self-criticism, common humanity the antidote for self-isolation, and a mindful or balanced approach to negative experience is the antidote for self-absorption.

When we are under stress, the body shuts down all unnecessary bodily functions including those associated with growth, such as digestion and reproduction. If your life is on the line, whether you are able to digest your food or conceive a child becomes immaterial. The heart rate increases, raising blood pressure. Stress hormones, including cortisol and adrenaline, are released and, although they help the body survive in a moment of danger, in the long-term they disrupt sleep and the development of new brain cells and we get stuck in cycles of negative thinking. When the sleep cycle is disrupted, many of the body's internal regulation systems that control appetite, learning, and mood are negatively affected and it can quickly become a vicious cycle.

It takes the body about 90 minutes to come back to homeostasis or balance after the stress response is activated, so if it is repeatedly being activated during the day the body doesn't have time to recover and bodily systems become disrupted with potentially long-term consequences for health and well-being.

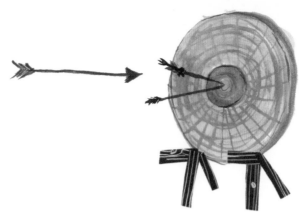

DRIVE AND SOOTHING

Like Threat, Drive is also a high stress state for the body to be in, and both states were designed to be engaged for only short periods, unlike the third, Soothing, which is when the body's growth and reproduction systems are engaged. **Rest and digest** is the opposite of **fight, flight, or freeze.** As well as bonding with others, play, creativity, and innovation are characteristics of rest and digest. To operate at our best, we want our emotion regulation system to be in balance and only spend short periods in Threat and Drive, with the majority of time in Soothing; unfortunately, this is often not the case and the opposite occurs.

In addition to fight, flight, or freeze, scientists have identified an additional stress response, **tend and befriend.** In times of danger there is an instinct to protect the young and vulnerable (tend) and connect with others (befriend). Just like fight, flight, or freeze, while the tend and befriend response can be really helpful it also can be activated inappropriately. For example, we may take care of someone else at the expense of our own needs or worry excessively about our children when there is no danger.

So practicing mindfulness, kindness, and self-compassion is one way of balancing our emotional regulation system regardless of whether the perceived threat is internal or external.

OBSTACLES TO KINDNESS AND COMPASSION

We generally find it easier to practice kindness to others because we can be afraid of practicing self-compassion, not least because of some of these common myths identified by Neff (see page 7).

IT'S SELFISH: It's common to think that paying attention or making time for ourselves is selfish, particularly if you are a parent or carer. However, we can't look after anyone else if we are not at our best physically and mentally. Just remember the safety instructions on an airplane to put the oxygen mask on yourself before helping anyone vulnerable. Neglecting our own well-being in favor of others is an example of the "tend and befriend" stress response (see opposite) being out of kilter. Van den Brink and Koster (see page 7) suggest actively cultivating a compassionate "we-together" mindset rather than "you-first" (self-sacrifice) or "me-first" (selfish).

IT'S SELF-INDULGENT: Self-compassionate people are more likely to engage in healthier lifestyle behaviors, such as eating well and exercising.

IT'S NARCISSISTIC: Self-compassion isn't a judgment or evaluation of self-worth like self-esteem, which can easily become narcissistic. Instead Neff describes self-compassion as a way of relating to the "ever-changing landscape of who we are with kindness and acceptance," especially when things don't go according to plan. Self-compassion is something that supports us when times are bad as well as good, unlike self-esteem where it is either high or low and the latter makes us feel worse.

IT'S A SIGN OF WEAKNESS: Self-compassion strengthens emotional resilience by improving emotional regulation, so you are better able to handle the ups and downs of life. A self-compassionate person will accept personal failings and mistakes and work to improve them. Being able to regulate difficult emotions means being better equipped to help others while still protecting yourself.

IT UNDERMINES MOTIVATION AND PERFORMANCE: In fact, it is the opposite— a self-compassionate person is motivated through curiosity and interest rather than a fear of failure and disapproval. When a self-compassionate person fails to reach a goal, he or she will be more willing to make adjustments and have another go. When they make a mistake, they will carry the learning forward and be willing to try again. In terms of motivating others, a self-compassionate person will motivate like a good coach, encouraging and supporting yet being honest about areas for improvement.

IT'S SELF-PITYING: Rather than feeling sorry for ourselves, self-compassion allows us to acknowledge and accept our suffering because we are able to hold it kindly. This is a more effective way of processing and moving through difficult experiences than suppressing them. Self-compassion also encourages us to connect to the universal experience of suffering that is a part of life. Whatever challenges we are experiencing, someone else will be experiencing similar. This doesn't undermine or minimize our own suffering, but instead helps us see that suffering is part of the human condition rather than personal to us, due to something we have done. Sometimes our suffering may be a result of factors outside of our control—for example, anxiety or depression. Therefore blaming ourselves or seeing ourselves as weak or foolish is not helpful. A compassionate response is more appropriate.

HOW CAN YOU CULTIVATE KINDFULNESS?

Christopher Germer (see page 7) has identified five pathways we can use to introduce self-compassion into our lives. You can focus on any one or combination of these when you practice. Practice can be meditating (formal) as well as more informally, that is by doing what you usually do but in a different way. This book provides instructions and suggestions for activities and practices in the five pathways for both forms of practice.

1. **Physically** (softening into the body, nourishing, resting, and relaxing)

2. **Emotionally** (soothing yourself, embracing and holding unpleasant emotions like a mother with a crying child)

3. **Thoughts** (allowing rather than judging, noticing how thoughts come and go like the weather)

4. **Relationships** (treating others as you would wish to be treated)

5. **Spirituality** (acknowledging and committing to what you value and what gives your life meaning).

In the practices section, which starts on page 35, there are a range of meditations to cultivate kindness and compassion for yourself and others. You can experiment with these as you work through the weekly prompts if you would like to. If you would like to try meditating with guidance, there are suggestions for free downloads on page 188.

The weekly prompts are an opportunity to experiment with cultivating kindness and compassion in your everyday life. The more we can integrate our practice, the more useful we will find it. The more you can view it simply as how you live your life rather than as something separate that you do with a view of achieving something, the more you will get out of it.

SUPPORTING YOUR ONGOING PRACTICE

Whether meditating or practicing informally, there are two main challenges with practicing. The first is remembering to do it and the second is sticking with it.

It is important to acknowledge that learning to do anything takes time. Habits are created through repetition and we've often built up a repertoire of unhelpful ways of thinking and behaving over our lifetime. Practicing mindfulness and compassion are not quick fixes or magic cures, but rather a way of cultivating the capacity to care. So the practice of practicing is your first opportunity to cultivate kindness to yourself, particularly when you forget, get disheartened, find it difficult or uncomfortable, are full of self-criticism and doubt and want to give up! This is all normal. However, there are some things you can do to support yourself whether you are formally meditating or practicing in everyday life.

FOCUS ON JUST ONE THING

If you try to do too many things at once you will get overwhelmed. Keep it simple and be realistic about the time you have available. Whether establishing a meditation practice or doing the weekly informal practices, try to reduce the number of choices you need to make each day.

MAKE AN INTENTION

For example, be present with your children or partner/friend (informal practice) or mindfulness of breathing (formal meditation) and decide **when** you are going to do it and for how long (for some tips on informal practice, see page 29, and for meditation, see page 37). If you just do something once or twice it's not going to make much difference—however, if you keep on doing something different, then you begin to lay down neural pathways in the brain (see page 14) and create new habits of thinking and behavior. Although each week has a new activity or practice, you can always continue

one for longer if you wish. Writing down an intention will make it stronger, more real, and also act as a nudge when you see it.

REFLECT ON WHAT YOU NOTICE

This is when we notice connections and gain insight, which helps reinforce learning and encourages us to keep going. We may think we will remember, but we are more likely to forget so making notes can be helpful.

TAKE CARE OF YOURSELF

It is counter-intuitive and therefore challenging to learn to turn toward what hurts us rather than pretend it doesn't exist. When we start paying attention to our experience, we may find it uncomfortable to see what is there—that is, notice the negative thoughts, feel the pain of sensations or emotions. It is important to make taking care of yourself your priority. It is wiser and safer to creep forward with baby steps, testing the waters of discomfort and then retreating as often and for as long as you need to. You can use the breath and the body (see page 43) to ground yourself or perhaps just do something nice for yourself (there are opportunities in the weekly activities to discover what self-care practices are most helpful for you). This is practicing kindness. Gritting your teeth and pushing through physical or emotional pain is not.

Feeling overwhelmed

If at any time you feel overwhelmed, just stop. We are peeling off some of our protective layers when we meditate and when we open our heart we can connect with long-suppressed hurts and pain which can be challenging. This is normal (but doesn't always happen) and is a recognized phenomenon that Neff and Germer (see page 7) call "backdraft." In the moment, stopping and doing grounding practices such as breathing through the soles of the feet can be helpful. However, sometimes we have to acknowledge that it is not the best time for us to be exploring this practice, particularly if we are going through a challenging time.

It is better to master new techniques when you are well, so they are already part of your life when you really need them. It is also better to learn new skills with small things that have less emotional charge, so do heed any cautions that I give in the practices.

MANAGING EXPECTATIONS

Whenever we practice, we are not chasing a particular experience and this is especially important with kindness and compassion meditations. When we meditate we do not expect to experience warm and fuzzy feelings. We usually feel nothing at all and that is okay. The benefits of regularly meditating on kindness will often show up in our daily life in terms of how we treat ourselves or other people rather than "on the mat." There is also no obligation or expectation to like or enjoy the practices—that can just create additional unhelpful pressure.

HELPFUL ATTITUDES

As well as an over-arching attitude of kindness, warmth, and tenderness, there are other attitudes that are cultivated by the practice, but we can also intentionally bring them to mind as we practice.

CURIOSITY: Practice being interested in what is arising—asking yourself *what* you are experiencing rather than *why*. If curiosity feels too much—how about just being interested. Immediately this shifts your mindset from one of resistance to approach or moving toward. Ask yourself "What am I noticing?" in the head, heart, and body when you feel good as well as when things are more challenging. Become familiar with the territory of your head, heart, and body whatever the emotional weather.

NON-STRIVING: It's easy to get attached to wanting a particular outcome, but this can box us in and prevent us being open to whatever else might be arising. We can also fall into the trap of constantly judging our experience and measuring it against some imaginary yardstick and then feeling disappointment if we are not where we think we should be. Notice when you are striving for a particular result—what does that feel like in the head, heart, and body? Become familiar with its qualities so you can pick them up more easily. What does the opposite of non-striving—just allowing things to be as they are—feel like?

ACCEPTANCE: This simply means allowing what is here to be here (since it already is whether we like it or not) without trying to get rid of it. What do you do when you have an itch or are sitting in an awkward position? You will naturally scratch the itch or adjust your position. This is normal, but sometimes there are parts of our experience that won't improve or get better. Then we can get stuck wishing things were different —resisting our experience. An alternative is to acknowledge its presence and turn toward it; stop fighting it and "befriend it"—get to know it better—how it manifests physically, and how it affects your emotions and thoughts. Acceptance is the opposite of resignation: a positive active step that takes courage.

PATIENCE: Change takes time. You have a lifetime to practice. It is unrealistic to expect you are going to be able to be kind to yourself, others, and the world 100% of the time. However, perhaps 10% of the time might be possible? Notice when you get impatient with yourself, tuning into how it feels and perhaps do a self-compassion break (see page 61). Every time you do something different you are helping yourself. This is why writing down what you have done and reflecting on what you notice is so useful. We have a natural negativity bias that means we will overly focus on what we haven't done at the expense of any positive experiences that we are not primed to remember, therefore writing down will help us remember *all* our experiences (good, bad, and boring) and consolidate learning.

NON-JUDGING: There's no point in noticing your experience and then giving yourself a hard time about what you see. Instead observe **how you are relating to your experience** —liking or not liking. What do you notice in your head (thoughts), heart (emotions), and body (physical sensations)? We can fall into the trap of judging our judging mind, so when that happens just notice it with a sense of kindness—"there I go again." When we notice our experience and how it manifests in the body, we have already stepped out of it and moved into an observing frame of mind instead of being caught up in the experience.

BEGINNER'S MIND: We can easily feel jaded about our experience. We tune out of it with a "been there, done that, got the T-shirt" mentality that prevents us experiencing what is actually happening. Instead, remind yourself that every experience is unique if you allow yourself the opportunity to be open and curious about it.

Your commitment to your practice will wax and wane and that is normal. When it falls by the wayside it will be waiting for you to pick it up again. Being ready and willing to do that is part of the practice.

REMEMBERING TO DO IT

If you want to establish a regular meditation practice, I recommend you do it at a regular time. Be intentional about choosing the time and reminding yourself with alerts if you need to. Where possible, try to establish a routine about what you are doing to reduce the number of choices you need to make. For more tips, see page 37.

One of the biggest obstacles to informal practice is remembering to do it once we get caught up in the busy-ness of the day. You can help yourself remember by:

- Tagging a practice to an existing activity. For example, being present with your children when you pick them up at school or bedtime; with your partner/friend at a mealtime. The more specific you can be, the better—so name the mealtime! If you can, schedule 2–3 opportunities to act as reminders. Of course, you will often forget but at some point you will remember and that is an opportunity to do the practice right then or at the earliest opportunity. It is important to keep making the intention and every time you forget is an opportunity for you to remember to practice, so don't lose heart or be self-critical.

- Creating a visual or auditory prompt that you associate with the activity/practice. For example wearing a particular piece of jewelry, setting a reminder on your phone, using a colored sticker in a strategic place, or making a particular color your prompt so every time you see the color red, for example, you do a practice. Be creative.

- Take the time to explore why you want to practice (see page 72) as this will help you make your practice a priority.

- Get into the habit of setting a regular intention as a way of strengthening your focus. You can do this at the start of each day—for example, it might be simply reminding yourself what you are noticing or cultivating that day (eg. How Am I Treating Myself Right Now Physically? See page 108) or perhaps it is simply setting an intention to "be kind to myself and others" throughout the day.

HOW KIND DO YOU THINK YOU ARE?

The Wheel of Life is a simple visual tool that is used to identify areas in our life that perhaps need more or less attention. It was originally developed by Paul J Meyer, founder of Success Motivation® Institute, Inc, and is a tool commonly used by professional coaches. Here I have adapted the concept into a Wheel of Kindness so you can identify the level of kindness and compassion you feel you currently offer to yourself, others, and the environment. As well as an overall "wheel," you can drill down a bit more in each domain if you wish.

HOW TO DO IT (these instructions apply for each wheel)

1. Rotate round the wheel and in turn, using a scale of 0 (low) to 10 (high) write down the degree of kindness and compassion you feel you currently give.
2. Mark your score on the relevant spoke.
3. Join up all the marks around the circle, as shown below.
4. Reflect on the resulting shape. Does it feel balanced or do some areas get lots more or less kindness than others? As well as discovering areas that would benefit from more attention, you may find that you are giving too much in other areas; this can show up particularly when we look at kindness to others.

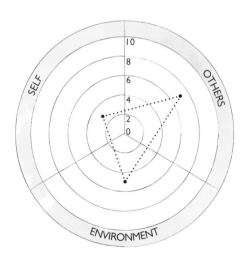

REMEMBER: When doing any reflection like this, it is important to do it without judging. It is simply a tool for giving yourself feedback.

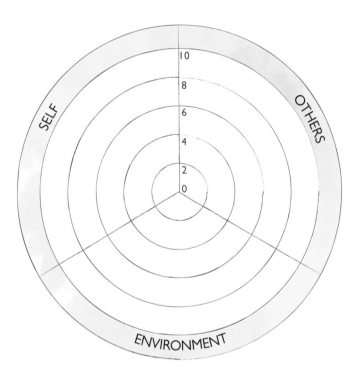

1. THE WHEEL OF KINDNESS

This wheel covers the three domains of kindness and compassion to **ONESELF**, **OTHERS**, and the **ENVIRONMENT**. How much care, kindness, and compassion do you think you give to yourself, others, and the environment? Reflect and mark on each spoke what you think. You can then drill down further and explore Self-kindness and Kindness to others overleaf.

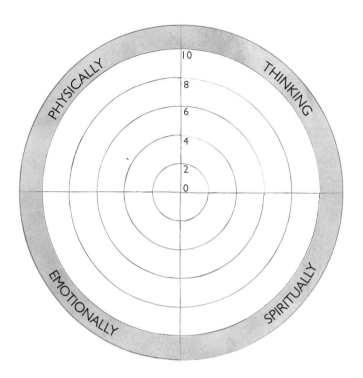

2. SELF-KINDNESS

This wheel uses the four of the five pathways to self-compassion identified by Christopher Germer (see page 23: physically/thinking/emotionally/spiritually—the fifth, relationships, is covered separately).

PHYSICALLY: How kind are you to your body? Do you take care of it by eating healthily, exercising, and resting regularly? Do you push it beyond its limits? How do you take care of it day in and day out—do you brush your teeth or hair roughly, for example?

THINKING: How self-critical are you? Do you set impossibly high standards? Do you judge yourself for your actions and/or behavior? What tone does your voice have? What kind of words and phrases do you use toward yourself?

EMOTIONALLY: How do you treat yourself emotionally? Do you self-soothe when things are difficult?

SPIRITUALLY: How much do you acknowledge and commit to what you value in life? Reflect and acknowledge where you are at as honestly as you can.

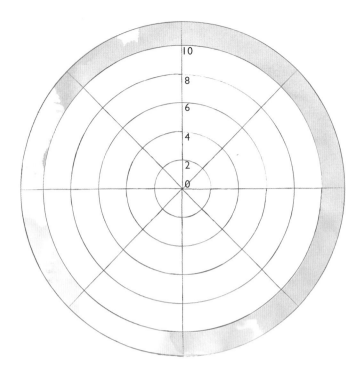

3. KINDNESS TO OTHERS

This wheel has blank spokes so you can insert specific names or categories according to your own circumstances. You don't need to fill in all the blanks, but as a minimum I recommend you include your partner (if relevant), family, friends, co-workers (if relevant), and strangers. You can break it down into individuals if you wish. "Family" can of course mean non-blood relatives—someone you consider as family. Look at your scores. Do you treat others as you would wish to be treated?

REFLECTION: What do you notice looking at your wheels? Are there are any surprises? Can you identify areas where you would like to increase your kindness and compassion score? Are there are areas where perhaps you need to pull back a little and perhaps not devote so much attention to?

It is important to acknowledge that our attention will fluctuate between the different domains and up and down depending on what is going on for us. This is okay. Knowing and being aware of this means we can make continual adjustments to live a healthy, balanced, kindful life.

MEDITATION PRACTICES

This section gives you practical tips for meditating, as well as instructions for some simple meditation practices. Whether or not you intend to practice formally, i.e. meditate, I'd encourage you to read this chapter as the information and reflections will support the more informal practices that make up the Weekly Activities that start on page 69.

HOW TO MEDITATE

Meditating regularly is one way you can cultivate kindfulness—by intentionally
paying attention to your experience as it arises without judging it, as well as
by intentionally cultivating particular qualities, such as kindness and compassion.

Meditation can be likened to going to the gym, except you are exercising your
muscles of awareness and giving your attention a workout. Just like going to the gym,
don't feel you have to *like* doing it. You may like it, but it's fine if you don't. It is
important you let go of chasing a particular outcome or feeling a particular way.
When you meditate, you are practicing being with whatever mind state comes up.
And when you meditate regularly you will experience them all—restlessness, irritation,
boredom, calm, bliss, anger…

Meditation is an opportunity to practice learning how to respond and be with
whatever arises in a relatively safe environment—for example, practicing with a minor,
albeit irritating itch on your nose, rather than something loaded with emotional charge.
Meditation teaches skills that can be generalized to everyday life. Regular meditation
can also change the brain and the body (see page 14).

Although when you meditate, kindness is implicit by the way you pay attention,
you can also meditate with the explicit intention of cultivating particular qualities
such as kindness, caring, connection, and friendship. The Cultivating
Kindness practices on page 63 are an example of this.
It is important to note that you don't have to
meditate in order to practice mindfulness or
compassion for yourself and others. You can also
cultivate similar qualities through informal practices,
that is, knowing what you are doing while you are
doing it. It is, however, often harder to practice
informally as it is easy to get caught up in the

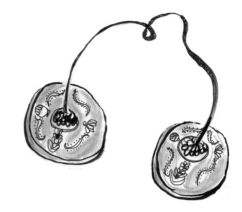

busy-ness of the day and forget your intention to practice. There is more about how to practice informally on page 29.

WHEN YOU MEDITATE: YOU ARE PRACTICING

- Noticing when your attention gets distracted
- Noticing what is pulling your attention away
- Letting go of the distraction
- Bringing your attention back to a focus
- Choosing where you want to place your attention
- Cultivating qualities such as curiosity, patience, letting go of striving, acceptance, gentleness, beginner's mind, and trusting in the process.

Just like exercise, meditating is something you need to do regularly for change to occur—little and often is what is recommended.

Practical tips for meditating

- Choose a place where you feel safe.
- Turn off your phone and remove other distractions.
- Set a timer if you need to be somewhere at a certain time—perhaps place it under a cushion/pillow so it won't give you are start when it sounds.
- Background noise is usually inevitable—it's all grist to the mill, so don't feel things have to be a particular way before you can meditate. Life rarely goes to plan so the more we can practice with this, the better!
- Review Taking Your Seat on page 38.

MAKING THE MOST OF YOUR PRACTICE

- Be realistic. Start with short practices of just a few minutes and build up from there.
- If you want to establish a regular practice, try to incorporate it into your daily routine. Choose a particular practice and decide a time and commit to this for a week, for example, so it's just something you do rather than having to make a choice about what to do and when each day.
- A little and often is better than longer and more infrequently.
- Be kind to yourself when you forget or life gets in the way. It is inevitable that there will be ups and downs and periods when you struggle to practice. You can always pick it up again at any time.
- Explore listening to guided practices if that's helpful (see resources on page 188). These can be particularly helpful if you are starting out.
- Let go of expectations. If you are constantly striving for a particular outcome, you will be judging your experience and measuring it against some imaginary yardstick and most likely you will fall short in your mind. Instead you want to approach each practice as if you are experiencing it for the first time and you don't know how it is going to unfold. This is beginner's mind where so many possibilities and opportunities await.

Most importantly, if at any time you feel very uncomfortable, panicky, or overwhelmed just stop immediately. You can always seek the advice of a professional or make the informal practices your focus. Meditation isn't for everyone or sometimes it is just not the right time for us to be doing it, and that's okay.

TAKING YOUR SEAT

When you meditate, your posture can either support or undermine your frame of mind. It's helpful to periodically notice how you are sitting during a practice, particularly if you are feeling dull or sleepy, and make any adjustments you need to.

You can meditate standing, lying down, walking, or sitting. If you are sitting, there's no need to assume any complicated positions, an upright chair is fine— however, if you are sitting or kneeling you may find it easier to use props such as cushions, blocks, or meditation stools. We are all different, so it's important to find a position that's right for you.

BEING GROUNDED AND CONNECTING WITH TOUCH POINTS

- If you are sitting on a chair, make sure that both feet are flat on the floor (you can always place them on a block or pillow, if necessary).
- If you are sitting cross-legged on the floor, make sure your hips are higher than your knees (you can sit on a block or a pillow to achieve this) and support your knees, if necessary, with pillows.
- If you are lying down, lie flat on your back with your legs outstretched (you can place a pillow under your knees) or with the soles of the feet flat on the floor and your knees up.

ALERT YET RELAXED

- When sitting, drop your attention to the lowest part of the body in contact with the floor and then move your attention up the body. When you reach the base of the spine as you slowly move up, imagine you are elongating the spine as you move from the lower back, through the middle back, upper back, back of the neck, and head. Slightly lift the crown of the head to the ceiling so the chin becomes tucked in.

EYES

- Your eyes can be open or closed. Experiment with both. If you are feeling sleepy, have your eyes open. If your eyes are open, drop your gaze down to the floor at about 45 degrees and have a soft, unfocused gaze.

It is inevitable that you will feel some discomfort when meditating, but remember practicing kindness extends to meditation and how you treat your body.

THE WANDERING MIND

It is the nature of the mind to wander so there is no point in trying to prevent it or stop thinking. At some point you will realize your attention has been hijacked and at that point you are in the present moment, so congratulate yourself rather than blame yourself! Acknowledge "thinking," perhaps notice what pulled you away, and then gently redirect your attention back to the focus, such as the breath or sensations in the body.

Of course your mind will wander again, so repeat these steps over and over. This is the practice—you are encouraging your unconscious to pick up the mind wandering, you are noticing your habitual patterns of thinking (what is on your mind), and you are practicing letting go of a distraction and choosing where to place your attention instead—and of course, practicing doing all of this with a huge dollop of kindness, thereby encouraging your unconscious mind to pick up when your attention wanders.

TUNING INTO THE BODY

Most people spend the majority of time thinking about their experience rather than feeling it. This disconnection from our physical experience may be because our body has let us down through illness or aging, or perhaps we don't like the way it looks. Uncomfortable sensations in the body are painful so we tune out from them. Unfortunately, this means we fail to receive essential feedback. The body has so much to tell us about how we are physically and mentally and so we can begin to reconnect by doing a body-focused practice like this one.

We can also use the body to process difficult emotions. Commonly we try to think our way out of emotional distress, but this problem-solving strategy works against us and actually compounds the problem and we get stuck in over-thinking or rumination. Instead we can shift our attention from the head and into the body and notice how the difficult emotion is manifesting in the body—whereabouts it is, how it feels, and how it is changing. When we do this we are taking a different stance to what is arising.

It also gives us an opportunity to practice being with sensations we don't like: the itch on the nose, for example. We can experiment with turning toward, and breathing with and into it as a way of dipping our toes into discomfort, although with relatively trivial sensations it teaches us skills that we can draw on if and when we experience physical pain.

We practice tuning into the body in informal practices (see page 98) as well as when we meditate.

WHEN THE BODY HURTS

Pain is your body's way of telling you that something is wrong. You might have injured yourself or have an illness, a headache, or toothache, or perhaps your body is simply aging and not functioning as well as it should. We often talk about "battling pain" or "beating pain," but this is cultivating an attitude of fighting and overcoming it—trying to make it go away—and it is this resistance to what is arising that is the main cause of suffering. However, sometimes there is nothing we can do to make it go away, so what do we do?

You do the opposite. You drop the resistance (since you can't stop it) and allow it to be present. You can turn your attention to it and become interested in it. What do you notice about your body? When we are in pain, the muscles usually tense up around the place that is hurting. We grit our teeth and jaw and brace ourselves against the pain, which creates further tension. There is often a story playing out about the pain—how bad is it? How long will it last? Is it getting worse? What does it mean? The story feeds the fear and our anxiety. We may stop trying to do things just in case it aggravates the pain and these limitations can create problems of their own and so our pain constrains us physically and mentally.

How you relate to your pain is something you can change and one way you can do this is by meditating. However, this isn't easy so always begin with the small discomfort like the aching shoulders or the itch on the nose. It's important to ground yourself in the breath and the body and use these as an anchor or place of focus and practice toward the pain in baby steps—maybe only turning your attention to it quite fleetingly before returning to the breath. You are staying there as long as you need to and then, if it feels okay, opening to the sensations of pain for a moment or two again, and so on. Practice kindness toward yourself by taking it slowly.

You can also practice this with the everyday hurts—a headache, toothache, or stubbing your toe, for example. The instructions remain the same:

* Notice the pain, acknowledge it, as well as noticing any resistance to it and acknowledging that too.
* Become aware of how you may be reacting to the pain—for example, tensing up around it.
* Ground yourself with the breath—perhaps imagine you are breathing in and out of the pain or anchor your attention on the breath in the chest or belly while at the same time having an awareness of the painful sensations.
* Be interested in the sensations themselves—what are they like? How would you describe them? Where exactly are they? Are they moving, still, changing, constant? Find out more about the sensations.
* **Remind yourself you are not trying to get rid of the pain.** You are practicing being with it—embracing it—since it is already here.

Soothe yourself in the way you'd comfort a crying child.

MINDFULNESS OF BREATHING

Tuning into your breath is often one of the first practices you learn when you begin meditating, but you'd be mistaken in thinking that it's only a practice for beginners. Mindfulness of Breathing is a great meditation on its own and it's also a versatile practice that you can do while you are out and about. The breath gives you an opportunity to practice right now, in this moment.

Never meditated? Become aware of the sensations of the breath. There's no need to think about the breath, but rather feel it entering and leaving the body.

Your practice has lapsed? At any moment tune into the length of the in-breath until it becomes an out-breath, and then with the out-breath until it becomes an in-breath.

Feeling stressed? Connect with the breath as anchor. As soon as you notice the busy mind pulling you away, ground yourself by imagining you are breathing through your feet on the floor.

In pain? Imagine you are breathing in and out of the place that is hurting.

Busy mind? Every time your attention wanders, you have the opportunity to see what is pulling you away before you bring it back to the breath. Most of the time it's just everyday nonsense, but if something is troubling us we can gain insight into what it is.

You can tune into your breath for a round or two or sit with it for an extended period of time. You can become aware of it sitting down, lying down, and standing up. You can tune into it when you are alone or in a crowd without anyone knowing what you are doing.

As a moving target, it requires a bit of effort to follow it. When our attention wanders (and it often will), the breath is an easy thing to bring our attention back to. We know it's always going to be there.

The breath changes according to our mental and physical state—we often hold it when we are stressed; the breath is more shallow and rapid when we are in pain, and slower and deeper when we are calm. Each one of us has a unique breathing pattern and the more familiar you can become with yours, the easier and quicker you will pick up subtle changes that give you feedback on your frame of mind as well as how you are physically.

TRY THIS

If you haven't done this before, I'd recommend sitting somewhere quiet where you won't be disturbed. Use an upright chair, if possible. Once you are familiar with the practice, you can experiment with doing it standing up, lying down, and when you are moving. You can do this practice for a couple of minutes or much longer. If you are new to this, start with a shorter time.

Begin to **become aware of your breathing**. Tune into the sensations of the breath entering and leaving the body. Where do you feel it most strongly? It's usually in the belly, the chest, or around the nostrils or upper lip. It can be helpful to choose one of those locations and rest your attention there. If you are having trouble noticing the sensations, just place a hand on your belly or chest to strengthen that felt connection.

Notice your breathing—is it short and shallow? Long and deep? A little bit irregular? There's no need to change the breath or breathe in any particular way (although sometimes just noticing the breath causes it to change and that's okay). Just let the breath breathe itself exactly as it is. Becoming familiar with your own breathing patterns is a helpful way of picking up when they change due to your emotional state or a physical injury or illness.

Sooner rather than later, your attention will be pulled away by your thoughts: *"Am I doing this right? What's for lunch? I wonder if it's going to rain later?"* And so on...This is normal! However, at some point **you will realize your mind has wandered** and this is

an opportunity to acknowledge "thinking," congratulate yourself for being present, and bring your attention back to the sensations of breathing. It is important to do this with a gentle kindness rather than beating yourself up.

Bring your attention back to the sensations of breathing. Staying with the in-breath for as long as it takes to breathe in. Notice that space as the in-breath becomes an out-breath and then stay with the out-breath for as long as it takes to breathe out and so on. Simply ride the waves of the breath as they come and go.

Continue for as long as you wish—noticing the sensations of breathing and bringing the attention back when it wanders.

Sometimes focusing on the breath can be tricky, particularly if you suffer or have suffered from breathing problems. If for any reason paying attention to the breath makes you feel panicky or anxious, just stop. You can always do a simple practice like imagining you are breathing through the soles of your feet on the floor instead.

There is a difference between thinking about the breath and noticing the sensations of breathing. We are interested in how the breath feels physically as it enters and leaves the body. Perhaps the belly expands and contracts, or the chest rises and falls, or perhaps we feel a cool draft of air around the nostrils. Notice and explore the felt sensations of the breath.

KINDNESS TO THE BODY

This meditation is an opportunity to practice intentionally tuning into the body and cultivating kindness and compassion toward your experience—that is, acknowledging it and allowing it to be there, rather than suppressing it or rejecting it.

Take your seat (page 38). You may want to do this meditation lying down but remember we are practicing waking up rather than falling asleep, so don't make yourself too cozy!

At the start, make an intention to be open to whatever arises and receive it with kindly awareness. Begin to **tune into the sensations of breathing.** Just notice how the body responds to the breath as it enters and leaves. Perhaps notice where you feel the breath most strongly.

When you feel ready, **expand your awareness** out to include the whole body. There will still be an awareness of breathing as a physical sensation but as you scan through the body noticing any other sensations—both internal and external—arising:

* Touch points of the body in contact with the surface that is supporting you
* A sense of temperature—warmth, coolness, hot, cold, or neutral
* Air touching the skin or different surface textures of fabrics
* A full belly if you've recently eaten or maybe an empty belly that is rumbling and grumbling
* Areas of tension or tightness—the shoulders, neck, and jaw are places we commonly hold tension
* Areas where you may feel a sense of discomfort or even pain (see page 41)
* Areas that feel soft and relaxed.

Remember, you are not looking for a particular experience or hunting to find something—it's about opening your awareness to receive what is present from moment to moment.

Notice how you are relating to what is arising: are you aware of a sense of liking or not liking, or perhaps you are neutral? Notice when and how you are resisting your experience. "Not liking" may manifest as a tightening or tensing around the sensation or perhaps a particular thought story or a negative emotion around it. There's no need to give yourself a hard time about judging or resisting your experience but, instead, just notice that it's something you are doing and remind yourself it's okay to allow yourself to experience this since it's already here. There's no need to pretend it's not there or push it away.

If you become aware of any emotions such as boredom, frustration, irritation, or perhaps their opposites, notice how they manifest in the body. What does the emotion feel like physically?

You can **intentionally cultivate warmth and gentleness by turning toward whatever is arising.** How do you do that?

Breathing into: You could play with the breath. You can breathe in and out of a strong sensation. Directing the breath and imagining you are breathing in and out of that location.

Breathing with: You might want to rest your attention on your breath in the belly or chest and making that the focus but at the same time having an awareness of the sensations in other areas of the body.

Turning toward: You could move in a little closer to the sensation: what does it feel like? How would you describe it? Is it staying the same or changing? Is it moving around? Get to know more about it, but with curiosity rather than an attitude of analysis. You might want to offer yourself some self-soothing words—"It's okay, let me feel this. It's okay" and perhaps place a hand over your heart if you'd like to.

Whatever options you explore, **remember you are not trying to make any part of your experience go away.** You are simply being with what is arising rather than pushing it away and any action you choose to take—such as scratching an itch—do it and know that you are doing it.

We are practicing breaking the automatic, unconscious cycle of reactivity ("scratching the itch") and responding with awareness, but it's essential to practice kindness rather than stoicism. Even just pausing for a second before scratching the itch—and knowing that you are doing so—breaks that reactivity.

Whenever your mind gets pulled away, which it will do (see page 40), acknowledge "thinking" and just bring your attention back to the breath initially before widening out to include the whole body once more. It can be helpful to come back initially to the sensations of breathing before widening out your attention to include all sensations in the body.

Every time your attention wanders, just bring it gently back without any judgment or drama. Cultivate kindness toward all aspects of your experience.

Continue in this way as long as you wish.

To finish, notice if there is a rush to get up and jump into your day. If there is, instead, pause and tune into the breath for a round or two.

If you would like to, this would be an opportunity to set an intention for the rest of your day (see page 76).

SITTING WITH HEART: SOFTEN, SOOTHE, AND ALLOW

This practice is one where the invitation is to intentionally connect with the heart—physically and emotionally.

With any practice like this, it is crucial to take care of yourself. To avoid feeling overwhelmed, anchor yourself by tuning into the body and the breath at the start of the practice (see page 46) and then periodically throughout the practice. If at any point it begins to feel as if you are becoming overwhelmed by your experience, stop immediately. If you are new to practice, always start by recalling smaller, more inconsequential experiences. It can be tempting to jump in and try to make difficult feelings go away, but that is counterproductive and neither mindful or kindful!

You may want to do this practice somewhere private where you won't be disturbed. Take your seat (see page 38) and spend a few moments connecting with the touch points of the body with the ground and the seat. Tune into that sense of being held and supported by the seat and the ground.

Then turn your attention to the body and tune into the whole body, getting a sense of the space you occupy and any felt sensations arising.

Narrow your attention to your breathing and take plenty of time to settle into the rhythm of following the breath as it comes and goes, bringing your attention back when it gets hooked by thoughts.

Place a hand over your heart or, if you prefer, slightly higher over the collarbone so you can feel the pulse beating in your neck. Narrow your attention so it is focused on the hand in contact with the heart. Remind yourself to bring a sense of kindness and gentleness to your experience.

Tune into the heart, resting in the heart space. Beating… pumping your life's blood around the body. Connecting to that felt sense of the heart alive within you. While you may feel something, there is no expectation to feel anything in particular.

If it feels okay, allow yourself to recall a difficult emotion or experience that you have had recently. Perhaps remembering the circumstances when you experienced the strong emotion. As you bring it to mind, just become aware of any accompanying emotions and physical sensations.

How is this memory manifesting in the body? What does it feel like it? Where are you experiencing the strongest discomfort? Wherever it is, make that your point of focus (as long as it feels okay).

Continue to be aware of the breath and, in your mind's eye, imagine you are directing the breath in and out of the discomfort—breathing into it.

Acknowledge the presence of the sensations; if you feel it, acknowledge your resistance to what is arising.

Breathing into it, breathing out of it. The breath is like the wind caressing and embracing you: **softening**, gentling, smoothing... Most of your awareness is resting on your breathing, but you still have an awareness of the sensations arising in the body. If you need to, shift your attention so it's 100% on the breath.

As you connect with the pain and discomfort, **soothe** yourself with words of kindness. These could be phrases of your own (see page 56) or simply "It's okay," "It's okay—let me feel this" or "We all struggle at times."

Continue to soothe yourself as if you would a hurt child. Murmur phrases and words of love and kindness. Allow whatever is present to be there—since it already is. The pain is here—touching into it, rather than pushing it away or pretending it's not there. Allow yourself to feel it.

Continue as long as you wish, breathing with your pain, your hurt, your unhappiness. **Softening** with the breath, **soothing** with your words and the warmth of the hand in contact with the body, **allowing** yourself to feel what is here.

Finish by tuning into the touch points of the body with the floor and the seat, and then expanding your attention to include sounds and the environment around you. Make sure to treat yourself gently after a practice such as this.

MOVING MINDFULLY

Being present when we move is a great opportunity to tune into the body and explore felt sensations and how they change. People who struggle to sit still or those who are feeling particularly anxious often find some form of movement practice is helpful.

Any form of movement can be an opportunity for practice: running, walking, swimming, pilates, to name just a few, and of course, the meditative movement practices such as yoga, tai chi, and qigong. Combining an existing form of exercise with practice is a good way to weave mindfulness into your day.

The challenge is first remembering to be mindful—particularly if you have a long established routine with your exercise. Therefore it's important to set a clear intention at the start of any mindful movement practice that this is what you are doing: choose a focus and perhaps also a length of time (roughly). You may choose to make just a specific part of your exercise mindful—this could be at the start, in the middle, or at the finish.

You may choose to use a pause as an opportunity to practice. To notice the body breathing hard, for example, if you've been exercising vigorously; tuning into how the body is feeling and noticing any areas that may be tense or even experiencing discomfort. You may choose to pause and tune into your surroundings—whether indoors or outdoors—widening your lens of awareness to include sights, sounds, and smells.

HOW TO MOVE MINDFULLY

There are different elements to moving mindfully.

ATTITUDES: For movement to be mindful, you need to intentionally cultivate the attitudes (see page 26) and in particular non-striving—letting go of having expectations about achieving a particular goal; beginner's mind—opening to whatever is arising and experiencing it as if for the first time (which it is since every experience is unique); curiosity—being interested in your experience, which encourages an approach rather than avoidance mindset; and of course kindness—kindness toward your body and how it is right now and also practicing kindness toward yourself—how are you treating yourself as you move? Do you berate yourself for "not being good enough"? Are your thoughts crowded with "shoulds"?

TUNING INTO THE BODY: Notice how it feels as it moves—movement creates stronger physical sensations, so there is more to "grab" on to. These sensations will change and move as the body changes position so the attention has to work a bit harder to keep noticing them.

If you are walking, begin noticing the sense of the feet in contact with the earth. You may then choose to expand your attention and become aware of the whole body as it moves. When we pay attention to the body and the sensations, we may notice how we are tensing muscles or perhaps we soften and relax into the movement.

When we move *with* our body rather than against it, we often find we are faster (but that's not the goal!) and because the body is less tense and more relaxed, it performs better and is less prone to injury.

YOUR RELATIONSHIP WITH YOUR EXPERIENCE: As well as noticing the physical sensations, the invitation is to notice **how you are relating to the sensations.** Is there a sense of liking, not liking, or perhaps being neutral? Becoming aware of how we are relating to our experience is an integral part of practicing. Whatever we notice is okay—we are not looking to like an experience or to make a neutral or negative experience positive. The story we are telling ourselves about the experience will impact on the body—for example, if we don't like it we are more likely to tense up against the perceived threat to our well-being.

DISCOVERING YOUR "EDGE": We also want to explore that point where a movement changes from feeling okay to not okay—called an "edge." We do this because too often if we experience pain or discomfort, we react by either pushing through it with gritted teeth or we hold back so we never see what is possible for us right now—in this moment. It could be that we can do more or perhaps less than the previous time we tried. The invitation is gently to explore this "edge," approaching it as if for the first time, letting go of preconceptions about how we think it will be and imagine we are breathing into it.

It's easier to notice when we reach our edge when we are moving more slowly and mindfully—for example, doing a yoga pose—rather than running flat out. So if running is your thing, you might want to explore this edge when you are stretching after your run.

VARYING YOUR FOCUS: Moving mindfully is an opportunity to experiment with narrowing and widening your focus, your "lens of awareness." I always recommend beginning with a narrow focus such as the sensations of the feet in contact with the ground and hanging out there for a period of time. Then you might widen your attention to include sensations in the entire body (including the breath), and then perhaps even farther to include the environment around you—the sights, sounds, and smells. You may choose to focus on one of these at a time or just open to whatever comes your way.

It's interesting to see what happens to your attention, depending on whether your focus is wider or narrow. If your mind is particularly busy, perhaps keep a tighter, narrower focus. Play with narrowing it back down and then widening again—dancing back and forth, playing with your attention.

LOOKING FOR OPPORTUNITIES: Be aware of the times within your day that you are moving from one place to another. As you go to the bathroom, get a drink, go to talk to someone in another room, take the stairs instead of the elevator; even moving from sitting to standing is an opportunity to come into the body and pay attention to all the different parts that are involved as the body moves from sitting to standing.

Choose one type of movement within your everyday such as walking to the bathroom or to the kitchen to turn on the kettle, or even just moving from sitting to standing up, and make an intention to do that as a practice. Keep it as specific as possible to help you remember to do it (but, of course you, will often forget).

WALKING VARIATIONS

Just walking: You can do this indoors or outdoors. Choose a short distance either up and down or in a circle and just walk with nowhere to go. It can be helpful to say silently to yourself "lifting shifting placing" as you lift and place each foot. Try:

- Experimenting with bare feet
- Closing your eyes for short periods, as long as it's safe to do so
- Synchronizing your steps with your breath.

Walking in the street: "Just walking" is often done slowly simply to remind ourselves that we are walking in a different way to usual. There is no reason you can't do walking practice at normal speed, but you will have to be careful not to fall into habitual patterns. Don't listen to any music and turn off your phone. Always keep your eyes open!

MOVEMENT FOR LIMITED MOBILITY

If your mobility is limited, you can explore micro movements—and even if it's not, limiting the movement can offer another dimension. If your mobility is limited, this is an opportunity to notice how you are with things not working as well as they have in the past; perhaps being with sensations of discomfort or even pain (see page 41).

PRACTICE 1: From a seated position with your hand(s) in your lap, tune into your breathing (see page 43), and when you are ready let both or one hand float palm up for the length of the in-breath and then palm down, let it float back toward your lap as you breathe out. The movement can be very small.

PRACTICE 2: Sit or lie, spread one hand out so there is space between the fingers. Place the tip of your index finger from the opposite hand at the top of the thumb. Tune in to your breathing. When you are ready, as you breathe out, slide the index finger down the side of the thumb to its base. As you breathe in, move the index finger up the side of the next finger and then as you breathe out, down the opposite side. Continue in this way moving up and down all the fingers and then repeat as often as you wish.

WHAT WOULD YOU LIKE TO HEAR?

Although cultivating kindness is implicit when practicing mindfulness, you can actively cultivate it through formal meditation such as loving kindness or self-compassion practices.

There are traditional phrases that are often used in loving kindness and self-compassion practices—for example, "May I/you/we be well/happy/free from suffering."

These phrases are conduits for our attention—a focus—in the same way we may focus on the breath or sounds or the body or something else. Our attention acts like a spotlight, strengthening our intention.

When we say the phrase, it's about opening to the possibility that in this moment, you in your life, the way it is right now, may be well, happy, or free from suffering. The attitude behind the words and the phrases is more important than the actual words.

FINDING YOUR OWN WORDS

We can make our practice more personal by changing these traditional words to something that resonates more with us. We can discover these words in different ways and I recommend exploring both the Reflective Meditation (see opposite) and the Free Writing Exercise (see page 59), as they often bring up different things.

Once you have completed these practices, pull out any words or phrases that strike a chord with you and make a note of them here. Say the words out loud. How do they feel in the body? Tune in.

Choose 2–4 of the words or phrases that resonate the most to use in practices like the Self-compassion Break (see page 61) and Cultivating Kindness practice (see page 63). I'd really encourage you to learn them by heart so that you can repeat them whenever you need to.

Remember:

- Keep it simple and easy to remember
- You can use single words rather than phrases
- You can use phrases such as "free from…"
- You can add qualifiers—for example, "as well as it's possible for me/you/we to be right now"
- They don't have to be perfect!

REFLECTIVE MEDITATION

This reflective meditation is an opportunity to discover what arises from your sub-conscious when your mind is settled. You may want to have a pen and a piece of paper to hand.

You will ask yourself two questions. The first is "What words would I like to hear every day for the rest of my life?" What we want to hear is usually something we want to experience. The second question is asking what needs do you have? These needs should be universal ones such as love, peace, safety, rather than for personal gain.

PART 1: Take the time to settle into your seat. Ground yourself by connecting with the touch points of the body—any places where the body is in contact with the seat or floor. Tune in to your breathing. Sit with the sensations of breathing long enough to settle.

When you are ready, silently ask yourself: "What words would I like to hear every day for the rest of my life?" Keep asking that question, or a variation of it, every so often without any expectations—just open up to whatever arises. It may be a felt sense, an image, a word, or a phrase. Just keep asking the question.

If you'd like to, write down the words you would like to hear. (You can turn them into phrases in the final part of the reflection.)

When you feel ready, move on to Part 2.

PART 2: Ask yourself, "What do I need?" "What do I truly need?" For example: "safe" becomes "May I be safe" or "May I be free from fear." Write down the words that come to you if you'd like to.

REVIEW YOUR WORDS AND CREATE YOUR PHRASES

When you are ready, take a moment to review all the phrases and words—perhaps saying them out loud and seeing how they resonate with you physically in the body. For example:

PART 1: The phrase "I love you" may become "May I love myself just as I am."
PART 2: The phrase "safety" may become "May I be safe" or "May I be free from fear."

Settle on 2–4 phrases that you would love to hear again and again. Write them here.

_____

_____

_____

_____

_____

_____

_____

_____

Explore the Free Writing exercise opposite and see what comes up through that.

Then pick out your favorite words and phrases from each exercise and write them up on page 60. Try them out in the Self-compassion Break (see page 61) or the Cultivating Kindness practice (see page 63).

FREE WRITING

This is another way to explore words and phrases that mean something to you. As with the reflective meditation, this exercise has two parts: Part 1 explores the words you would like to hear and Part 2 explores what it is you truly need.

The rules are simple:

- Set your timer for 2 minutes
- Start each sentence with the suggested words
- Don't stop writing
- Don't edit
- If you run out of things to say in Part 1, keep repeating the question
- Keep going until the timer sounds
- Set timer for another 2 minutes and do Part 2. Same rules apply.

PART 1: I would like to hear every day for the rest of my life the following words….
(then shorten to: I would like to hear…).
Continue on as many sheets of paper as you need.

PART 2: What do I need? What do I truly need? (then shorten to: I truly need….).
Continue on as many sheets of paper as you need.

SELF-COMPASSION BREAK

This practice was developed by Neff and Germer (see page 7) and designed to be done in the moment at times of difficulty. It only takes a minute or so and can be done any time, any place, and without anyone else being aware.

It's helpful to do the practice regularly when things are going okay, so you become familiar with the structure and doing it becomes second nature—something you do periodically throughout your day—then you will naturally call on it when you need it. There are suggestions for how to remember to do this on page 29.

The self-compassion break is made up of different stages, each with an intention that can be made into a phrase (you can adapt the words as you wish). The phrases can be repeated slowly together:

"This is a moment of suffering,

Suffering is part of life,

May I be kind to myself,

May I give myself the compassion I need."

Don't get too caught up in finding the perfect words or worry if you forget them—it's the intention behind the words that is most important. If you would like to, you can place the palm of your hand on your chest or belly as you repeat the words.

STEP 1: A MOMENT OF SUFFERING

Acknowledge that this is a moment of pain and suffering. Tune into the felt sensations in the body. What sensations are arising? Where are they? If you are not aware of anything, that's okay. There's no need to go hunting for anything. What emotions are present? Simply notice how it is without creating a story around it. Other words might include "This hurts," "This is stressful," "I'm in pain."

STEP 2: SUFFERING IS PART OF LIFE

Widen your awareness out from your own circumstances and connect with others in a similar situation. Bring to mind anyone you know specifically or a particular group of people and perhaps remind yourself that you are all in this together. This pain you are experiencing comes with the territory of being human. Often our suffering is a result of factors beyond our control. It's just the way it is rather than a personal failing. Other phrases might be "pain is part of being human," "I'm not alone in experiencing this."

STEP 3: MAY I BE KIND TO MYSELF

Offer yourself words of kindness and love. You might want to take some time to find words that particularly resonate with you (see page 56). If you find it hard to come up with a phrase, Germer and Neff suggest thinking of words you would say to a friend or loved one in difficulty. Other phrases might be "May I be safe," "May I be strong." You might remind yourself that you are doing your best. Things often don't go to plan or unfold as we would like them to, but it's better to respond to mistakes and failures with kindness and compassion rather than self-criticism and judgment.

STEP 4: MAY I GIVE MYSELF THE COMPASSION I NEED

Actively remind yourself that you are cultivating self-compassion. Germer and Neff suggest alternatives phrases such as "May I accept myself as I am" or "May I learn to accept myself as I am." You can also substitute "May I" with "Can I"—experiment and see which one resonates most with you.

The self-compassion break should be not be done with the expectation of making your hurt disappear. It won't. It is about acknowledging what is here; what you are experiencing rather than suppressing it and pretending it's not there or creating an overly dramatic story around it. You are connecting with that sense that you are not alone—whatever it is you are experiencing there will be others who have experienced it in the past, are experiencing it right now, and will do so in the future. Finally, you are offering yourself comfort and support. Treating yourself with self-compassion in times of distress has numerous benefits (see page 15). The more you can do this practice, the easier you will find to do it in times of difficulty.

CULTIVATING KINDNESS MEDITATIONS

Loving Kindness is a traditional Buddhist meditation where qualities such as friendship, kindness, caring, and kinship are cultivated along with acknowledging the connections that exist between all of us. We can change the way we relate to what is happening to us by paying attention in a particular way (mindfulness) and by cultivating a sense of connection with us (loving kindness).

When we feel connected to another person they cease to be "other" and separate. Instead of being labeled "a difficult person" or "a stranger" we see them as an individual, as someone's son or daughter, or perhaps as someone with the same color hair as us or with a similar taste in music. Someone with the universal desire to be happy and free from suffering.

The following practices are drawn from the traditional loving kindness meditations, and although they have been adapted, they are still about establishing an intention and cultivating an attitude: an intention to offer kindness, connection, warmth, and friendship to oneself and others, and intentionally cultivating those attitudes. This is done by silently repeating certain phrases, which reinforces attention and concentration.

THE PHRASES

You can use the words/phrases suggested on pages 66–7 or you can discover the words you really would like to hear (see page 56).

- Decide on some words and stick with them—don't keep changing them!
- Anchoring the words to the breath can be helpful
- Substituting "may" with "can" might feel gentler and more open to possibilities—experiment and see how it feels to you

- Say the phrase silently and slowly
- Don't expect to feel anything, but give yourself time to let the words settle. You don't want to gabble the words without any sense of them.

HOW YOU RELATE TO WHAT IS ARISING

The practice is about how you are relating to the experience rather than the content:

- Notice what you resist
- Notice what you tune out from
- Notice what you turn toward.

Be awake to reverberations and ripples within the body—notice if any emotions arise.

Remember you don't have to like it. When you do a meditation like this, don't expect to feel any warm fuzzy feelings—often we feel nothing, but the fruits of regularly cultivating kindness are often seen in everyday life. Cultivating kindness is not about trying to fix or change ourselves or another person, but rather connecting with ourselves and them.

CULTIVATING KINDNESS FOR YOURSELF AND A LOVED ONE

Before you can offer kindness to others, you have to be able to offer it to yourself. Although this can feel self-centered and self-indulgent, it is always worth reminding yourself of Germer's recommendation that you give yourself the attention you need so that you don't need so much attention.

Because it can feel challenging just to offer kindness to yourself, this practice includes offering it to someone we care about or who has supported us in some way; someone who has our best interest at heart (it could even be a much-loved pet). By thinking of someone who has been positive in our life, it becomes easier to connect with similar feelings toward ourselves. Although if it still feels challenging, continue with "we" rather than "I." There is no rush.

Sometimes you may experience strong resistance during this type of practice, so it's essential to spend time at the start grounding yourself in the breath and the body and be willing to return there at any point you need to. If the practice feels challenging at any point, just stop.

TRY THIS

Take your seat (see page 38).

Take a moment to decide on the person you want to offer kindness to.

If you are using your own words/phrases, perhaps have them written down and to hand in case you don't remember them.

Take a few minutes to tune into the breath and ground yourself in the sensations of breathing. Locate the place where you can feel your breathing most strongly and remind yourself that this is your home base—the place to come back to at any point you need to.

Take your attention to your eyes, mouth, jaw, and allow them to soften.

Bring your loved one/supporter to mind. Hold a sense of them in your heart and mind. Begin to silently repeat the following words (or use your own):

"May you be kind to yourself and others."

Silently say the words slowly and pause before repeating. Notice how you respond to them—is there a sense of liking, not liking, or simply neutrality? Notice any ripples or resonance.

Repeat the phrase a number of times. Then picture yourself with your loved one/supporter and change the words to:

"May we be kind to ourselves and others."

As before, repeat the words slowly, letting them go as if you were dropping a pebble down a well, listening for any reverberations.

"May we be kind to ourselves and others."

Repeat the phrase a number of times. Then offer these words just to yourself:

"May I be kind to myself and others."

Feel free to experiment with the alternative: *"Can I be kind to myself and others?"*

Notice any feelings of resistance, such as tension or tightness in the body. If it feels too strong, it's fine to revert to offering kindness to both yourself and your loved one/supporter.

"May I be kind to myself and others" or *"Can I be kind to myself and others?"*

Remember to keep checking in with the breath and the touch points of the body.

Finally, offer these words of kindness to yourself, your loved one/supporter, and adding any other friends, family members you'd like to:

"May we be kind to ourselves and others."

Finish by bringing your attention back to your breath for a few rounds.

CULTIVATING KINDNESS FOR SOMEONE IN DIFFICULTY

We can feel quite helpless in the face of another person's suffering so this variation is an opportunity to offer words of support, warmth, and friendship to someone you know who is struggling.

They may be going through a tough time at school, work, or home, or perhaps experiencing physical or mental illness, or maybe they are caring for someone else. Of course they won't be aware of your good wishes. You are offering them without any expectation of receiving anything back. Possible phrases might be:

"May you take care yourself."

"May you be kind to yourself."

"May you be as well as it's possible for you to be right now."

Follow the previous instructions to set up the practice and then picture the person who is struggling. Offer them your chosen words, silently repeating them as often as you wish.

At the end, widen your circle to include your original person, yourself, and any other people you would like to offer these words to. Always include yourself at some point in the practice.

Finish by tuning into the breath for a round or two.

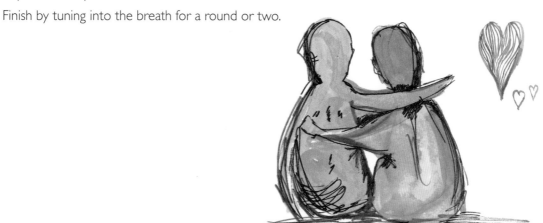

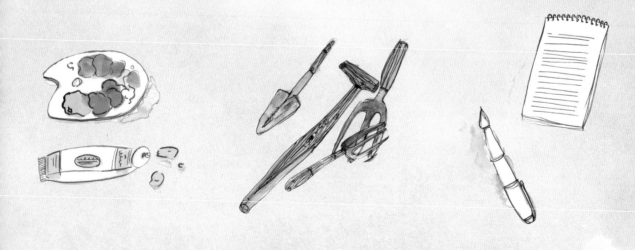

WEEKLY ACTIVITIES

Ideally work through the activities and practices in order. It's best to focus on just one activity or practice at a time and do it for a few days—forgetting and remembering is all part of the practice. There will be some that resonate with you more than others and you can make a note of these on page 186. However, it is always worth revisiting a practice that you've previously dismissed at some point. In time you will find that you are naturally implementing certain practices in your life without even thinking about them.

WHAT DOES KINDNESS MEAN TO YOU?

Kindness is commonly defined as the quality of being friendly, generous, and considerate. Sounds good, doesn't it! However, I think kindness is much more than those three words. Digging a bit deeper into what kindness means to you can be a helpful way to explore creative ways to integrate it into your life.

TRY THIS

For this practice, first take a few minutes to sit quietly, not as a formal meditation—just allow yourself to settle into a reflective space. Set a timer for 3 minutes, then pick up a pen and in the space opposite or in a journal start a sentence with the words:

Kindness is ....

Begin each sentence in the same way. Don't think about what you are writing, don't edit or score through your words. Just keep going without stopping until the timer goes off. If you run out of things to say, just write whatever comes out, even if it is something like "I don't know what kindness is" or even "kindness is not ..."

You may end up writing about kindness toward yourself, it may be more about other people, or it might be about the environment. Don't try to direct your writing in any particular way. The idea is to drop below your thinking mind and just let whatever is present flow through the ink of the pen!

Once the timer has finished, pause for a moment or two and then read what you have written. What do you notice about the content? How does it feel in the head, heart, and body as you read your words? Are there any surprises? There is no right or wrong definition—this is about what kindness means to you personally. If particular words or phrases resonate with you, pull these out and make a note of them separately. These can form the basis of a daily intention (see page 76).

FRIENDLY GENEROUS HELPFUL altruistic
affectionate gentle COMPASSIONATE caring
tender HELP understanding neighborly CONCERN
thoughtfulness WARMTH courteous kind-hearted

REFLECT ON WHAT KINDNESS MEANS TO YOU

_____

_____

_____

_____

_____

_____

_____

_____

_____

_____

_____

_____

_____

_____

_____

CONNECTING WITH YOUR "WHY"

If you want to establish a kindness practice and keep it going day after day,
week after week, and month after month, you have to have a sense of why
you are doing it and why it is important to you? Connecting with your
"why" will make your practice an active engagement that you choose to do, which
will help you make it a priority in your life.

Your "why" is your personal vision. It's like an ever-present guiding star that you
can check in with periodically. Your vision is your big picture. It's important to connect
with your heart and body when exploring what is meaningful to you—your mind may
say one thing, but the heart can feel very differently.

Dropping below the thinking mind can be hard, so it can be helpful to explore
your "why" in two different ways— through a reflective meditation and also
through a writing practice.

MY WHY: A REFLECTIVE MEDITATION

Find a place and time when you won't be disturbed and take your time to settle into your seat (see page 38). Begin by connecting to your breath (see page 43). When you feel ready, silently ask yourself the following questions or variations of them:

How do I want to live my life?
What kind of person do I want to be?
What do I want to feel in my life?
What is important to me?

It may help to have a printout of the questions to hand, but this activity is not so much about answering those specific questions as connecting to an over-arching sense of who you are and what kind of person you want to be, so feel free to change the words if you prefer.

Whatever words or phrases you are using, repeat them every so often, just asking yourself the question and seeing what arises. We are not looking for specific answers. Sometimes there may be an image, a felt sense, a word or phrases, and sometimes nothing at all, and that's okay.

Continue for 5–10 minutes and then finish by settling your attention on your breath once more and connecting with the touch points of the body.

While you are in this quiet space, take a moment to jot down what came up for you. Don't worry about making sense of it. Connect with the breath and touch points of the body and read what you have written. As you do so, notice what arises in the body and the heart. What resonates with you?

MY WHY: A WRITING PRACTICE

Exploring the same questions from the reflective meditation through
a writing practice can sometimes take us below the thinking mind.

Here we change the questions so that they become a statement.
How do I want to live my life? becomes *I want to live my life….*
What kind of person do I want to be? becomes *The kind of person I want to be is…*
What do I want to feel in my life? becomes *I want to feel…*
What is important to me? becomes *It is important to me that….*

The instructions are simple—gather together plenty of paper, a pen, and a timer.
If you want to, write the statements down before you start. Set your timer for
5 minutes, then begin writing. Don't stop until the timer goes and don't edit, cross
out, correct spellings, etc. Keep repeating the statements or variations of them. You may
go off on a tangent as you write and that's okay. Just see what happens.

   Once the timer goes, lay down your pen. Connect with the breath and touch points
of the body and read what you have written. As you do so, notice what arises in the
body and the heart. What resonates with you?

_____

_____

_____

_____

_____

_____

_____

_____

MY VISION

Pull out key words and phrases from both these practices and use them to write up your vision. Keep it in a positive voice and in the present tense. Come back to it periodically and re-read it. You may want to edit it from time to time.

_____

_____

_____

_____

_____

_____

_____

_____

_____

_____

_____

_____

_____

_____

_____

_____

_____

_____

_____

CREATE A DAILY INTENTION

By creating a daily intention to practice kindness, it will become a habit. Just as we can strengthen a muscle by repeatedly exercising it, we can also cultivate new, more positive ways of thinking by repeatedly carrying out the new action, thereby laying down neural pathways in the brain. As psychologist and author Rick Hanson says, "Neurones that fire together, wire together." The challenge is remembering to repeat the intention often enough so that it becomes a habit.

For example, if we would like to be less judgmental of others or less self-critical, we might create a daily intention to be kinder to others and to ourselves. Note, it is more helpful to create a positive statement such as "May I be kind to myself" than, for example, "May I be less self-critical."

Change takes time. Ideally decide on one intention and keep it going for at least seven days. Let go of any expectations about the outcome and focus solely on the intention. There are two parts to this—first strengthening the mental habit of remembering and, second, implementing the intention.

IDEAS FOR INTENTIONS

Below are some examples of intentions, but use words or phrases that resonate with you. There is no need for fancy phrasing!

MAY I BE PRESENT WITH MY EXPERIENCE

MAY I BE KIND TO OTHERS

MAY I BE KIND TO MYSELF

MAY I TAKE CARE OF MYSELF

TIME TO REFLECT

Once you've decided on your intention, reflect on what it means in practical terms. For example, what does being kind to yourself really mean? Do you mean physically taking care of yourself or perhaps replacing self-criticism with self-compassion? Try to keep your intentions as simple as possible initially. You may find it helpful to review what came up for you in Week 1, *What does Kindness Mean to You?* (see page 70).

TIPS TO HELP YOURSELF REMEMBER

- Write down the intention along with a start date and the date that you'd like to review it (at least seven days). The act of writing it out will itself strengthen it and be a powerful motivator.
- You may also want to write out your intention on a small piece of card—perhaps stick it somewhere at home or at work where you will see it regularly, or inside your wallet where you will notice it every time you come to pay for something.
- Choose an activity that you do more than once a day that you can tag as a prompt to help you remember. It might be at mealtimes or when you are making a hot drink, or perhaps on your journey to and from work, or when you are putting on your shoes or brushing your teeth… Every time you do the activity, repeat the intention to yourself. It's important to acknowledge that you will forget most of the time, but at some point in your day you will remember and that's an opportunity to repeat the intention. Even if you only remember as you are about to fall asleep, repeat it then.
- Tie a piece of yarn or put an elastic band around your wrist—every time you see it, repeat your intention silently to yourself.

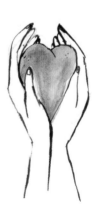

DAILY INTENTION

MY INTENTION:

_____

_____

START DATE:

_____

REVIEW DATE:

_____

REFLECTIONS:

_____

_____

_____

_____

_____

_____

_____

_____

_____

_____

_____

SLOW DOWN TO BE KIND

How often do you carry out an act of kindness? If rarely, what is it that stops you?
For many people, it's not that they don't want to be kind, they are just too busy.
Even if we notice the opportunity to do something positive, we may feel we don't
have the time to actually do it. For example, we might rush past someone who clearly
looks lost or not find time to get in touch with a friend in need.

The fact that you are less likely to help someone out if you are in a hurry was
supported by a famous "Good Samaritan" study (Darley & Batson, 1973) carried out
with a group of religious students at a seminary. The degree of urgency that was
induced in the students affected the likelihood of them stopping to help a "victim" in
need. Overall 40 percent offered some help to the "victim." In "low hurry" situations,
63 percent helped, in "medium hurry" situations 45 percent helped, and in "high hurry"
situations only 10 percent helped.

When you are busy or in a hurry, how does it affect your actions and behavior in
relation to others? Bring this into awareness over a period of time.

TRY THIS

When you notice the busy-ness—the physical and mental feeling of rushing—
experiment with pausing. Acknowledge how you are feeling and how it is affecting you.

Play with intentionally offering a random act of kindness when you have all the time in
the world, when you are busy, and when you are harried. What do you notice? It may be
easier to start when you have plenty of time, but I'd encourage you to experiment with
doing it when you are rushing as well.

An act of kindness doesn't always have to be toward a person—
you can, for example, be kind toward the environment by picking up
a piece of trash or removing an obstruction from a path.

NOURISHING NATURE

Spending time outdoors is a great way of being kind to yourself mentally as well as physically. As well as lifting your mood, connecting with nature—the sky, the landscape, the weather, and the seasons—is a way of gaining some perspective. You can also use the senses as a way of bringing yourself into the present moment rather than getting stuck in the past, which is history and can't be changed, or in the fantasy of the future.

TRY THIS

Take a walk outdoors—in a park or the countryside, by the sea or a lake. The walk can be for just a few minutes or much longer. Remember to let go of any expectations about how the walk should make you feel.

Leave your phone at home or at the very least put it away. This is an opportunity for you to commune with nature. Engage the senses: sight, sound, touch, smell, and even taste, if it's possible. You may do this systematically or simply make an intention to open to whatever comes into your awareness. Listen to the birdsong, feel the wind, notice the insects, hear the crunch of leaves underfoot, breathe in the scents or perhaps the experience is less pleasant. Just notice.

Periodically take a moment to tune into the body. How is your body responding to the environment? How is it connecting with the earth beneath your feet; the temperature; the weather? What do you lean into (yummy) or tense up against (yuk)? What do you notice?

Make a walk like this part of your routine—do it whatever the weather and regardless of the mood you are in. When we revisit the same place throughout the year, we notice the small subtle changes that occur as time passes and the seasons change, and we notice too how our experience is in flux in the same way.

REFLECT ON CONNECTING WITH NATURE

_____

_____

_____

_____

_____

_____

_____

_____

_____

_____

_____

_____

_____

_____

_____

_____

_____

_____

_____

_____

_____

_____

WHAT DOES UNKINDNESS TOWARD YOURSELF FEEL LIKE?

What we feel subconsciously may be very different to what we think intellectually. This exercise is an opportunity to explore what unkindness toward yourself looks and feels like. We can't change behaviors until we become aware of what we are doing and acknowledge how it affects us.

TRY THIS

Take a moment to sit, connecting with the touch points in the body (see page 39). Then set a timer for 5 minutes. Begin writing, *"I am unkind to myself when I …"* Don't stop writing, or cross out or edit your words. Don't worry about grammar, spelling, and punctuation, or whether you are making sense. Begin each sentence with the same phrase. When the timer goes, pause and read through what you have written. Notice what arises for you. Do a self-compassion break (see page 61) if it would be helpful.

Pull out specific thoughts, actions, or behaviors and list them below your sentences. Notice whether they are internal (thoughts) or external (actions and behaviors). Are there any surprises?

Choose one action or behavior and make an intention to bring it into awareness in everyday life.

- Notice when you do it—how do you feel in the head, heart, and body?
- Notice what happens beforehand—is there something that prompts the behavior?
- Can you offer yourself some compassion and self-kindness at this point? How about afterward?
- Experiment. Play with making an action or behavior less unkind or neutral in the first instance rather than trying to do a total flip to kindness. Change takes time.

REFLECT ON WHAT YOU DISCOVERED

_____
_____
_____
_____
_____
_____
_____
_____
_____
_____
_____
_____
_____
_____
_____
_____
_____
_____
_____

WHAT DOES SELF-KINDNESS LOOK LIKE TO YOU?

Last week you explored ways in which you are unkind toward yourself. This week is an opportunity to explore what being kind toward yourself looks and feels like.

TRY THIS

Take a moment to sit, connecting with the touch points in the body (see page 39). Then set a timer for 5 minutes. Begin writing *"I am kind to myself when I …"* Don't stop writing, or cross out or edit your words. Don't worry about grammar, spelling, and punctuation, or whether you are making sense. Begin each sentence with the same phrase. When the timer goes, pause and read through what you have written. Notice what arises for you. Do a self-compassion break (see page 61) if it would be helpful.

Pull out specific thoughts, actions, or behaviors and list them below your sentences. Notice whether they are internal (thoughts) or external (actions and behaviors). Are there any surprises?

Choose one action or behavior and make an intention to bring it into awareness in everyday life.

- Notice when you do it—how do you feel in the head, heart, and body?
- How does it influence what happens next?
- Once you become familiar with integrating this self-kindness behavior from your list, choose another.

REFLECT ON WHAT YOU DISCOVERED

_____

_____

_____

_____

_____

_____

_____

_____

_____

_____

_____

_____

_____

_____

_____

_____

_____

_____

_____

_____

_____

_____

ACKNOWLEDGING THE GOOD IN OTHERS

When someone we care about does or says something stupid, we often get
irritated and angry. We often blame them and might cast back a litany of their
faults and remind them of occasions when they have let themselves or others down.
This doesn't make anyone feel great and can undermine an individual's self-esteem.
Next time, why not try something different.

Instead of berating them, think about the individual's good qualities that you appreciate.
Reflect on occasions when they have offered kindness to people or helped others,
including you, in some way. This might be in words or actions. Focus on occasions when
their intentions came from the right place, regardless of the outcome.

You might want to take some time to reflect and then write your thoughts
down as a list or even a letter that you might read out or give to the person
concerned, or you can just share your thoughts with them. Just writing the list
can remind us that this is a person we love and care about, regardless of what
it is they may have done or said. It's not about pretending they haven't
done something that has upset you, but rather reminding you of
the bigger picture.

CREATE A FAMILY GAME

Create a jar for each family member. Every time someone does
something that is noticed or appreciated by another family member, they write it down
(it can be signed or anonymous) and pop it in the person's jar. If they are signing it, they
might want to include how it made them feel as well.

From time to time, take turns reading aloud what is written on one or more slips of
paper. Mix it up and be creative as possible. Depending on the ages of the children, get
them involved in decorating and labeling jars.

REFLECT ON ACKNOWLEDGING THE GOOD IN OTHERS

ACKNOWLEDGING THE GOOD IN YOURSELF

This practice is a variation of the one in Week 8, but instead of acknowledging the good in others, it's about acknowledging the good in yourself. Human beings have a natural negativity bias, particularly toward ourselves. Too often we ignore our good qualities and attributes or those times when we did something positive rather than negative. Noticing and acknowledging the positive things you already do will help to remind you to do them more often. As you start cultivating new behaviors you can acknowledge those too.

Write down a list of as many of your good qualities, attributes, and behaviors that you can think of. They can be one-offs or things you often do. Include things you do for yourself as well as for others.

Some examples might be:

- I usually make eye contact with people.
- I stopped to help the woman who was lost, even though I was late for work.
- When the service at the cafe was really slow today, I handled it well. Instead of getting frustrated, like I often do, I took a deep breath and noticed the tension in my shoulders and how tired I was. I realized that everyone else was probably as hot and tired as I was and I promised myself a relaxing bath when I got home.
- I usually give my full attention when someone is talking to me.

Be as specific as you can, so rather than writing "I'm kind to others," write down an example such as "I carried my elderly neighbor's shopping up to her apartment last week."

Don't worry if you find that your list is short. The more you do this activity, the better you will get at noticing how much good there is in what you do for yourself and for others.

MY GOOD QUALITIES, ATTRIBUTES, AND BEHAVIORS

1. _____

_____

2. _____

. _____

3. _____

_____

4. _____

_____

5. _____

_____

_____

_____

_____

_____

_____

_____

_____

THE BODY BAROMETER PRACTICE

This is an informal practice that was developed by mindfulness teacher and author, Trish Bartley. The inspiration for it is the old-fashioned weather barometer that measures air pressure to give an indication of forthcoming weather. In this practice we tune into the body to read our own "emotional weather" and find out how we are faring.

Once you can acknowledge if you are feeling under the weather, stressed, tired, or anything else, you are in a better position to make a choice about what you can do to take care of yourself in the best way possible.

I recommend you do this practice regularly and when you feel good as well as in times of difficulty. It can be done any place and at any time and no one need know you are doing it.

TRY THIS

Tune into the body and ideally the trunk (the chest or belly or somewhere in between). This is because we usually experience the physical sensations of stress and strong emotions in the torso. You can place a hand there if you wish.

You may need to do this a few times before you identify the location where you commonly feel strong sensations in times of stress.

Then regularly tune into this location at different times. As you do this, you may become aware of quite subtle sensations. You will become familiar with your own body's "weather" signature and thereby pick up early warning signs. These can give you a signal that something is stirring long before you become aware of it intellectually in the mind.

Week 10

When you notice this you can:

Either tune into the breath or do the practice on page 132 to help you hold whatever is arising.

Or you can simply stay with the sensations, noticing them moment by moment, being with them as they are.

Sometimes you may prefer to choose one option over another and that's okay.

It's important to always remember to take care of yourself. Don't feel you have to stay with any strong sensations. Sometimes a wiser choice is to take your attention to the breath or the feet on the floor.

Cultivate your own Body Barometer and make an intention to tune into it periodically throughout your day as well as at any times of difficulty.

REFLECT...

_____

_____

_____

_____

_____

_____

_____

_____

_____

_____

_____

WALKING WITH KINDNESS

There are many opportunities in the day for walking practice (see page 54).
This variation invites you to incorporate a kindness element to it.

This is a practice to do somewhere there are people. They may be people you know
or complete strangers. You might be walking down a street or through a park... You
can do it for a minute or two or longer, depending on the time you have available.

TRY THIS

Walk and know that you are walking. Tune into the body and particularly the soles
of the feet.

After a period of time, widen your lens of awareness (see page 53) so you maintain
a sense of the feet in contact with the floor, but you also are aware of the people
around you.

Every time you pass someone or someone catches your attention, silently offer
some words of kindness such as "May you be well" or another word or phrase. You
can find out more about finding your own words and phrases on pages 56 and 63.

You are offering these words without an expectation of anything in return. You
are simply giving.

You don't have to offer the words to every single person. Just connect with anyone
you wish, when you wish.

You may choose to narrow your focus back into the body and the feet on the
floor from time to time and that's okay.

Notice what arises for you in the head, heart, and body.

REFLECT ON WALKING WITH KINDNESS

_____
_____
_____
_____
_____
_____
_____
_____
_____
_____
_____
_____
_____
_____
_____
_____
_____

PAY IT FORWARD

This practice encourages ripples of kindness to spread to others in a similar way to a random act of kindness (see page 79), but it has an additional element. The principle is simple: rather than expecting or asking someone to "pay you back" when you show them kindness, you encourage them to "pay it forward," i.e. do a similar act of kindness for someone else who then pays it forward, and so it continues—the kindness and appreciation ripple out to more and more people.

To help give you ideas for ways you can pay it forward, it may be worth exploring what kindness means to you (see page 70). However, this practice is about responding to whatever is arising right in front of you, rather than planning what you are going to do.

Opportunities to pay it forward might include:

- A stranger is struggling with bags at the station and there's no elevator. Pay it forward by offering to help.
- Someone falls down in the street. Pay it forward by stopping to check whether they are okay rather than walking by.
- Someone in the line ahead of you has trouble paying for their goods for whatever reason. Pay it forward by offering to foot the bill.

Accept the person's thanks, smile, and invite them to pay it forward. They may do or they may not—and that's their choice. You can only control your own actions, not anyone else's.

REFLECT ON HOW IT FELT TO PAY IT FORWARD

_____

_____

_____

_____

_____

_____

_____

_____

_____

_____

_____

_____

_____

_____

_____

_____

_____

_____

_____

_____

EXERCISING KINDFULLY

Exercise, along with diet and sleep, is generally accepted as one of the three foundational pillars of health and well-being. It raises the heart rate, makes blood flow faster, and floods the body with mood-enhancing endorphins—it has the potential to be a self-kindness practice benefiting overall well-being simply because of this.

We can also be more intentional about making exercise an opportunity to practice kindness, particularly if the body is not working as well as we would like. At moments like this, practicing kindness toward the body, with all its creaks and moans, comes into its own. Whether we are doing a specific type of exercise or simply walking across the room, we can practice moving kindfully.

TRY THIS

Choose one form of regular exercise and make an intention to incorporate a few minutes of mindful awareness into it and, in particular, offer yourself kindness before, during, and after the exercise.

First consider whether you have properly prepared your body for the exercise you are about to do? For example, if you try to run 10k without allowing your body to build up its strength and resources, you are not practicing kindness.

During the exercise, how are you treating your body? Are you pushing it beyond reasonable limits? Notice that edge between stretch (moving outside your comfort zone) and strain (moving beyond your body's capabilities in this moment) and keep as much as possible within the stretch zone.

Week 13

Are you giving your body what it needs in the way of hydration and nourishment before, during, and after you exercise?

How are you treating yourself mentally? What story are you telling yourself? If you notice you are commonly motivating yourself with self-criticism, have a look at the practice on page 142.

How do you take care of yourself after you have exercised? From drying your body after showering, to eating well to replenish your energy and allowing your body adequate rest to recover. Are you rough or gentle? Are you consciously giving your body what it needs and deserves? Just notice.

We only have one body and it is often only when it lets us down that we notice how much we take it for granted. If you let your body down, you are increasing the likelihood of it letting you down. Invest in your future, take care of your body.

Find out more about how to move mindfully on page 51.

SOFTEN AND LET GO

What do you do when you don't like your experience? The most common reaction is to brace ourselves—we tense the body against the perceived threat. It might be against the cold or rain, or against unkind words or a physical threat. All these micro movements done day in and day out, over and over again, add up and can affect how we feel mentally and damage our body physically, as muscles become tight and stiff. Instead, explore how you can treat your body more kindly.

TRY THIS

Periodically throughout your day tune into your body—simply noticing how it is.

- Notice where your shoulders are—are they pulled up around your ears? Perhaps they are caving in as you hunch over your desk or computer.
- How about your head? Notice the forehead—are you wearing a perpetual frown or creases of anxiety?
- What do you notice about the jaw—is it clenched or soft?
- Where is the chin—is it jutting forward, straining the neck?

Begin to pay attention and notice whereabouts in the body you commonly hold that tension.

Next time it rains or it's cold, notice the body bracing and tensing against it and intentionally encourage the muscles to relax; play with breathing in and out of that area. Do this at anytime you notice the body tensing up against your experience.

Or take a few minutes and simply focus on the out-breath, letting the body go each time you breathe out.

It takes time to train yourself to respond in a different way so be patient.

REFLECT ON LETTING GO OF TENSION

_____

_____

_____

_____

_____

_____

_____

_____

_____

_____

_____

_____

_____

_____

_____

_____

_____

_____

Week 15

STAND UP FOR YOUR BODY!

How many hours a day do you spend sitting hunched over a computer,
in a position that certainly isn't kind to your body? How we sit can create
tension in the body. The more we can be less sedentary and more active
in the workplace, the better.

An international group of experts was recently invited to provide recommendations
by Public Health England and a UK community interest company (Active Working
CIC). Their report highlighted the growing body of evidence that sitting still for long
periods increases the risk of getting a range of chronic diseases such as obesity, type 2
diabetes, and high blood pressure. Their recommendations were published in the
British Journal of Sports Medicine and include:

- Work toward getting at least two hours a day of standing and light walking during
  working hours, and eventually work up to a total of four hours a day.
- Avoid remaining in a static standing or sitting position for long periods.
- Take regular breaks from screen work to protect your eyes.

When you are sitting or standing, experiment with adjusting your posture so you are
working with your body rather than against it. Picture an imaginary thread running from
the base of the spine all the way up along the back, the back of the neck, and the back
of the head. If you gently tug on this thread, the crown of the head would rise and the
chin become slightly tucked in. As the spine straightens, the shoulders drop and the
chest opens.

Make sure your chair and desk are at the correct height and support you the
way you need. You can experiment with standing desks and different types of seating,
but be aware that your body may need a period of adaptation so look at phasing
in any changes.

Week 15

TRY THIS

- Get up and talk to a co-worker rather than sending an email or picking up the phone
- Walk up the stairs rather than taking the elevator
- Set a timer to remind you to move your body every 20 minutes if possible
- Do some seated stretches (see page 134)
- Take a walk at lunchtime
- Walk part of your commute at the start and/or end of the day—get off public transport a stop earlier or park your car farther away
- Arrange meetings away from your desk.

What else could you do?

THE SPIRIT OF APPRECIATION

When you appreciate someone, let them know about it. The person who shared this practice with me chooses one person in the workplace each week who has gone above and beyond in some way. He sends them an email saying he has noticed their good work or the way they handled a situation, or whatever it was, and compliments them.

I asked him whether he ever gets a nice email back. "That doesn't matter," he said, "The point isn't for them to make me feel good. It's about creating a feel-good factor for them, which in turn makes them want to make others feel good. So they then do exactly the same thing with someone else and so the appreciation ripples out."

This is a great practice to do in the workplace or with family and friends. Keep your compliments genuine, and give them when they are well-deserved. It may feel a little strange at first so notice any resistance and how that feels in the body and play around with the language you are using to find something that resonates with you.

You can deliver the appreciation by whatever means is most appropriate. Experiment and see what happens.

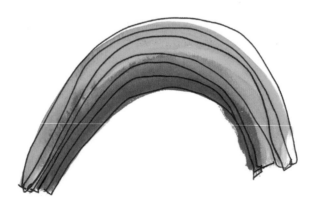

REFLECT ON SHOWING APPRECIATION

WHAT ARE YOU LEARNING TO LOVE?

This self-kindness practice was inspired by a poem called *Imperfection* in which the poet, Elizabeth Carlson, explores how she is learning to love her imperfections.

Many of us have things we don't like about ourselves. It may be some physical aspect due to genetics, illness, or aging, or perhaps we have certain personality traits that we wish were different.

Instead of rejecting these parts of yourself, can you instead learn to love them? Or if that feels a step too far, perhaps learn to tolerate or simply not dwell in aversion or meanness to them.

TRY THIS

Pick one thing that you don't like about yourself and practice this as best you can. Imagine seeing yourself from a different perspective—through someone else's eyes; be curious. What would someone who loved you say about this part of yourself that you don't like?

This is a practice you can do over a period of time, choosing different characteristics if you like and remember that we are all "work in progress" and a practice like this is often the work of a lifetime.

Use the page opposite or a journal to reflect on the feeling that came up for you.

REFLECT ON LOVING YOUR IMPERFECTIONS

DO SOMETHING THAT'S NOT ON A LIST

In the poem *Imperfection*, which I mentioned in Week 17, Elizabeth Carlson also writes eloquently about moving from a life of doing—crossing off items one by one—to a life where she'd rather waste time listening to the rain or "lying underneath my cat learning to purr." Of course there are always going to be things we have to do, but too often the to-do list dominates our life to the exclusion of all else.

Notice how you feel when your to-do list is not completed. Do you feel a sense of compulsion to complete it regardless of the cost to yourself? Being a slave to a list is not cultivating kindness. We create our own to-do lists so being willing to be flexible and let go of demands and build in time for just being is essential to cultivating self-kindness. Can you let go of the tyranny of your to-do list? Make time for finding your own equivalent of "learning to purr."

What would you rather do that doesn't involve crossing something off a list? Some examples of "just being" might be:

• Sitting listening to the birds or the wind and rain
• Stroking a pet— feeling the texture of the fur
• Cuddling a child—connecting to the warmth of the body and your two hearts beating
• Pausing and opening the senses and becoming aware to whatever is present

Pick one thing you'd rather do and practice it as best you can. This is a practice you can do over a period of time, choosing different activities.

REFLECT ON "JUST BEING"

_____

_____

_____

_____

_____

_____

_____

_____

_____

_____

_____

_____

_____

_____

_____

_____

_____

_____

_____

_____

HOW AM I TREATING MYSELF RIGHT NOW PHYSICALLY?

We can't do anything differently until we become aware of how things actually are, but too often we don't pay attention. We don't acknowledge the reality of things, so we might not actually be aware of how we treat ourselves.

If we do notice a harsh thought, we may think it doesn't matter—telling ourselves it's just that once. However, psychologist and author Christopher Germer talks about how a moment of self-compassion can change your day and a string of these moments can transform your life.

Over the next three weeks, we are going to start noticing how we treat ourselves **physically**—the way we look after our body; **mentally**— the way that we're thinking; and **emotionally**— this is partly to do with thoughts, but also how we nourish ourselves physically and spiritually.

This is an opportunity to acknowledge how things really are—the positive, helpful ways you treat yourself kindly as well as the less helpful ways. As always, when you are doing a reflection like this, hold what you discover lightly and with a sense of gentleness.

Week 19

Notice how you treat your body in different ways.

- Are you gentle or rough when you brush your teeth? How about when you wash, shave, or moisturize? Notice how you touch your body.
- How do you feed your body? Do you give it the nourishment it needs or do you feed it with junk?
- How about when you exercise? Do you push yourself beyond what you are capable of? How do you treat yourself if your body is performing below par? Do you let it recover or push through and keep going despite everything?

This is an opportunity to explore what practicing kindness toward your body actually means. What does it feel like? What does practicing unkindness toward your body feel like? What do you do to yourself?

Write down what you notice. Be as specific as possible, using concrete examples of words, and specific examples of actions and behaviors—both kind and unkind.

You may like to do this exercise over an extended period of time, adding information as you notice it.

REFLECT ON HOW YOU TREAT YOURSELF PHYSICALLY

_____
_____
_____
_____
_____
_____
_____
_____
_____
_____
_____
_____
_____
_____
_____
_____

HOW AM I TREATING MYSELF RIGHT NOW MENTALLY?

We don't usually notice our thoughts—they happen unconsciously, driving our actions and behaviors and influencing our mood, and vice versa. Much of our negative thinking results from the way we treat ourselves mentally—the words and phrases that dominate our self-talk and the tone of voice we "use" when we think.

Here the invitation is to notice, when possible, the inner critical voice as you go about your day. What is it saying to you? Are there particular words or phrases that are very familiar to you? Do these remind you of anyone from the past?

If there is any sense of feeling panicked or overwhelmed by memories, then feel free to stop if you need to. If it feels okay, explore tuning into the sensations of the breath and any touch points of the body to help keep you grounded in the moment. Of course, you may still get pulled away by your thoughts but as soon as you notice that happening bring your attention back to the breath and the body.

In what tone of voice do you hear the thoughts? I have a self-righteous indignant thought tone that as soon as I hear it in my head is a useful red flag that my thinking is skewed!

Although it is easier to notice the meanness as it's louder and stronger, remember to pay attention to the kind thoughts too. There's no need to judge the judging thoughts either—the first step is always simply to notice whatever is arising. It's often easier to notice after the event rather than in the heat of the moment and that's okay.

How do you practice self-kindness in your thinking? How about the less kind ways? Be as specific as you can when you reflect, but hold what you discover lightly and with a sense of gentleness.

Week 20

You may like to do this exercise over an extended period of time. Adding information as you notice it.

Notice how you speak to yourself. How could you reframe things to be kinder to yourself? Notice the specific words you use mentally, write them down and experiment with re-phrasing them.

I SHOULD DO BETTER THAN THIS.

I'M DOING THE BEST I CAN.

WHY DO I ALWAYS MESS THINGS UP?

EVERYONE STRUGGLES AT TIMES.

REFLECT ON HOW YOU TREAT YOURSELF MENTALLY

_____

_____

_____

_____

_____

_____

_____

_____

_____

_____

_____

_____

_____

_____

_____

_____

_____

_____

_____

_____

_____

_____

_____

_____

HOW AM I TREATING MYSELF RIGHT NOW EMOTIONALLY?

Our emotions are closely tied to our thoughts—the story we tell ourselves may make us feel a particular way such as ashamed, angry, or compassionate and kind. We can also nourish ourselves emotionally or spiritually by the way we look after ourselves—giving ourselves the time we need to rest, but also to pursue what interests or inspires us.

Ask yourself what feeds your soul? Are there particular activities or behaviors you do or have done in the past that nourish your spirit?

Here the invitation is to notice, when possible, how you are treating yourself emotionally. Just as with thinking, you may find it harder to notice when you treat yourself with positive emotions such as kindness and compassion, but don't give up!

How do you practice self-kindness emotionally and spiritually? How about the less kind ways? Be as specific as you can, but reflect on what you notice with gentleness, reminding yourself we are all works-in-progress.

What acts of self-kindness or its opposite do you commonly employ? Do you take time out for yourself? What hobbies or activities do you do? If there are ones you've given up due to other demands, explore whether it's possible to pick them up again. If you have family responsibilities, you may need to negotiate with a partner or family member to help you do that. It is important to remember that none of us can keep giving to others without giving something to ourselves as well.

You may like to do this exercise over an extended period of time, adding information as you notice it.

Write down the positive ways you practice kindness—nourishing your spirit. Make a list of things you are doing already as well as those on your wish list that you'd like to do.

REFLECT ON HOW YOU TREAT YOURSELF EMOTIONALLY

_____

_____

_____

_____

_____

_____

_____

_____

_____

_____

_____

_____

_____

_____

_____

_____

_____

_____

_____

Week 22

WHAT WOULD YOU LIKE TO BE DIFFERENT?

This week we're going to look back at what you've discovered in Weeks 19–21.
You can set an intention to actively cultivate the positive behaviors you have
noticed about the way you treat yourself physically, mentally, and emotionally.
It is always easier to continue to do something you are already doing than
introduce something new.

TRY THIS

Choose one of the positive behaviors you have noticed and make a daily intention to
practice it as best you can. If you didn't notice any positive behaviors, then reflect on
how you might do one of the unhelpful behaviors in a kinder way.

For example, if you push through pain when you exercise, make an intention to
tune into your body and notice when you are reaching your edge—that boundary that
feels like your limit. Instead of pushing through it, experiment with hovering around it
and easing back if necessary. Notice how you feel afterward.

You may like to enlist the help of a friend or partner as sometimes it can be hard to
see our own behaviors clearly. You could reciprocate and each support the other by
checking in and encouraging each other.

Write your chosen behavior down in the space opposite, along with the date and
your intention to practice it regularly. Don't choose more than one behavior—you will
just get overwhelmed and give up.

Of course you will forget, and that's okay! Every time you remember you've
forgotten is another opportunity to practice if you can in that moment or at the
earliest opportunity.

Practice it for a period of time—ideally a minimum of a week—and reflect on what
you notice.

You can always choose another behavior to actively cultivate once you have been
doing the first one for an extended period of time.

DAILY INTENTION

POSITIVE BEHAVIOR: _____

_____

DATE: _____

_____

INTENTION: _____

_____

REFLECT: _____

_____

_____

_____

_____

_____

_____

_____

_____

_____

_____

_____

_____

_____

HOW DO YOU TREAT OTHERS?

This practice is an opportunity to bring into awareness the way you interact and treat people. It is simply about paying attention to your usual behaviors and bringing an attitude of kindness to what you notice—noticing and acknowledging how things actually are, but without giving yourself a hard time if they aren't as you expected. There is often a mismatch between how we think things are and how they actually are.

TRY THIS

Make an intention to notice how you treat people. It is helpful to narrow this practice down to a specific group, for example family, co-workers, people who serve you in stores and cafés, or even one specific person such as a partner or family member. It is more fruitful to do this reflection over a period of time with the same group, rather than chopping and changing. You can choose a different group another time.

Decide on the scope of your observations. Make an intention to bring kindly awareness and simply notice how you interact. Remember, you are simply noticing your habitual patterns. Next week we will look at experimenting with doing things differently. Some suggestions for the type of things to be aware of:

- Are you present with others?
- Are you multi-tasking—checking your phone or emails or something else?
- Are you day-dreaming or lost in thought?
- Do you make eye contact?
- Are you rushing on to the next thing?
- Are you hearing what is being said to you?
- Are you responding to what is being said to you?
- Do you go out of your way to help people?
- What stops you helping someone?
- How do you shake someone's hand?
- Do you interrupt people?

Make notes opposite, being as specific as you can be.

REFLECT ON HOW YOU TREAT OTHERS

OBSERVATIONS:

_____

_____

_____

_____

_____

_____

_____

_____

_____

_____

_____

_____

_____

_____

_____

_____

_____

_____

TREATING OTHERS WITH KINDNESS

This practice follows on from the previous one, where you spent a period of time noticing how you treat others and from this you will have a picture of the typical patterns that you employ. Some of these may be less helpful than others.

TRY THIS

Reflect on your observations from last week and choose one thing you would like to experiment with doing differently. There's no point in being over-enthusiastic and choosing multiple things as you will forget and then feel as if you have failed.

Decide on the one thing you'd like to do differently as a way of offering kindness to others. Make an intention to practice this. You will probably need to keep on reminding yourself of your intention—see page 76 for some tips on this.

Be kind to yourself when you forget.

Continue with this one action for an extended period of time as this will help strengthen it as a new behavior.

Notice and reflect how implementing this new action makes you feel and notice any observations around how it impacts on your interactions with others.

REFLECT ON TREATING OTHERS WITH KINDNESS

_____

_____

_____

_____

_____

_____

_____

_____

_____

_____

_____

_____

_____

_____

_____

_____

_____

_____

_____

APPRECIATE "SMALL" ACHIEVEMENTS

Acknowledging and celebrating our achievements is a positive way we cultivate kindness toward ourselves. What is considered a personal achievement will vary for each individual, but the idea is to give the small things we manage to do or complete as much weight as the big things, like passing a test or getting promoted.

Sometimes just getting up in the morning and facing the world can feel like a huge accomplishment, or not snapping at a partner when we feel angry, or maybe getting through that pile of washing and ironing that has been piling up... Nothing is too small or insignificant, but these are the achievements we often dismiss.

The typical "big" achievements deserve attention too, but it is often the smaller ones that we miss and merit being brought into awareness and acknowledged. When we start paying attention and notice how much we actually have done, we feel a sense of accomplishment and well-being that encourages us to do more and boosts our self-esteem.

TRY THIS

You can do this periodically throughout the day or in the evening take a moment to reflect over your day.

- What felt like a struggle?
- Notice when you feel a sense of relief, elation, satisfaction. What were you doing? How did it feel physically in the body?
- What thoughts if any did you notice?

Make a list of your achievements and reflect on them on the page opposite.

REFLECT ON "SMALL" ACHIEVEMENTS

_____
_____
_____
_____
_____
_____
_____
_____
_____
_____
_____
_____
_____
_____
_____
_____
_____
_____
_____

HALFWAY REVIEW

It's always useful to pause and review where you are at. It is an opportunity to reconnect with your "why" (see Week 2), review any intentions or goals that you have set, and make any adjustments. This is an opportunity to reflect on what you are noticing about yourself and your behavior/actions.

It's important to acknowledge that life rarely goes according to plan and being willing to be flexible and respond to how things actually are in your life rather than how you wish they were is at the heart of practice. So, bearing that in mind, be willing to make adjustments without giving yourself a hard time.

What is your biggest takeaway around practicing kindness toward yourself and others so far?

_____

_____

_____

_____

_____

What would you like to be different if anything going forward?

_____

_____

_____

_____

_____

REFLECTIONS SO FAR...

_____

_____

_____

_____

_____

_____

_____

_____

_____

_____

_____

_____

_____

_____

_____

_____

_____

_____

_____

ACCEPTING KINDNESS FROM OTHERS

Many of us find it easier to offer kindness to others than accept it for ourselves. In Week 1 there was an opportunity to reflect on what kindness means to you— you might want to remind yourself what came up for you.

TRY THIS

This practice is a chance for you to be open to the many opportunities when people offer **you** kindness. It might be from family, friends, co-workers, neighbors, or strangers.

Notice and acknowledge when someone does you a kindness—it might be something they say or something they do for you or for themselves so you don't have to; it might be as simple as holding a door open or genuinely asking how you are today.

A person may do something for you that doesn't go according to plan—or that isn't as you would have done it yourself. When this happens, notice the judging thoughts and remind yourself of the intention—the motivation behind the action. That is what is important.

The invitation is simply to notice and acknowledge these moments—allow yourself to accept them with the warmth and care with which they are offered. Sometimes you may want to notice, too, how it feels physically in the body and emotionally. Also notice your thinking—particularly any thoughts that undermine the kindness, such as questioning motives or thinking that you don't deserve it.

Just acknowledge and receive whatever is being offered with kindly awareness and without judgment.

REFLECT ON ACCEPTING KINDNESS

MAKE A DATE WITH YOURSELF

It's very easy to get so caught up in the busy-ness of life that we don't make time for ourselves. I first came across "The Artist Date" in Julia Cameron's *The Artist's Way*, and while I never do these dates enough myself, I love the idea of them. We all need some space to replenish ourselves mentally, so think about what activity could do that. Aim to schedule a date with yourself once a month, if possible, or once a quarter. Protect this time for yourself and make sure those close to you understand how important it is so they support you—and you in turn can reciprocate by supporting them to do something similar.

You might choose an activity that you haven't done in a long time, or perhaps something that you've always wanted to try. It may be as simple as leaving yourself time in your diary that is not scheduled so you can respond to how you feel in that moment, or it might involve going somewhere or booking something in advance. I recommend you don't involve other people, otherwise you may lose sight of the fact that this is *your* date to try and compromise and fit in with others.

If nothing comes to mind, take a moment to reflect—perhaps closing your eyes and asking yourself "What feeds my soul?", "What nourishes me mentally?"

Keep asking yourself these questions, or variations on them, and be open to whatever arises. Tune into the body and listen to your heart. Write down any ideas that come to mind—however silly or impossible you think they may be. Pick one and schedule it. Do it!

REFLECT ON MAKING TIME FOR YOURSELF

BEING KIND TO THE ENVIRONMENT

Everything we do impacts on the world around us: the clothes we wear, the goods we buy and how we dispose of them, the energy we consume, the way we travel, how we look after birds, insects, fish, animals, trees, and plants, and how we manage the habitats they need to survive—the list goes on.

While it can be tempting to think that what we do won't make a difference, we are all interconnected and nothing will change unless each one of us takes responsibility for our own actions.

Reflect on how you practice kindness to the world around you. Take some time to notice all the things you currently do—as well as the things you don't do.

TRY THIS

Make a list of positive actions that you could take. There are some ideas opposite and space to add your own. Choose one action from the list and make an intention to implement it. Some actions may be easier than others, so perhaps start with one that is easily achievable. Continue with that one thing until it becomes a regular habit—something you do without thinking about it, then introduce another action, and so on.

It will take a while to start doing things differently and there will be times you forget, but don't give up! The sea is made up of trillions of drops of water, the beach is made up of trillions of grains of sand… everything you do has an impact.

Week 29

SOME SIMPLE IDEAS

PICK UP AND DISPOSE OF TRASH WHEN
YOU SEE IT

CHECK WHAT PESTICIDES YOU ARE USING IN THE GARDEN AND
SWITCH TO ENVIRONMENTALLY FRIENDLY ONES, WHERE POSSIBLE

TURN OFF LIGHTS WHEN YOU LEAVE A ROOM

ALLOW A SMALL AREA OF GARDEN TO GROW WILD TO CREATE
ESSENTIAL HABITATS FOR INSECTS AND WILDLIFE

TURN YOUR HEATING DOWN A DEGREE OR TWO
AND PUT A SWEATER ON INSTEAD

PUT FOOD AND WATER OUT FOR THE BIRDS IN WINTER

TURN APPLIANCES OFF, RATHER THAN LEAVING THEM ON STANDBY

CARRY A "KEEP CUP" FOR DRINKS ON THE GO

REDUCE YOUR SINGLE-USE PLASTIC

What else could you do?

_____

_____

_____

_____

_____

_____

_____

_____

WHAT DO YOU NEED RIGHT NOW?

This is a simple self-care practice you can do as many times as you like throughout the day. It is an opportunity to pause, notice, and acknowledge how you are feeling in the head, heart, and body and asking yourself what it is that you need right now.

You can do this practice when you are alone, in a crowded room, with your eyes open or closed. Create an intention to do it daily—see page 76 for some tips.

STEP 1

Check-in with your head, heart, and body, and acknowledge whatever is present. This is about noticing whatever is present in your thoughts, emotions, and physical sensations. There may be nothing obvious and that's okay— there is no need to go hunting for something! You may just have an overall feeling, rather than distinct strands of experience. Sometimes you may have thoughts or feelings that you don't like, or that you think are inappropriate, but it is important to acknowledge those too since they are all part of your experience in this moment.

STEP 2

Tune into your breathing. Narrow your attention on to your breath and follow it for a few rounds—staying with the length of each in-breath and out-breath.

STEP 3

Silently ask yourself, "What do I need right now?" Repeat the question a few times and just notice whatever arises. Allow your body to tell you what it needs.

Continue with the day and, if possible, implement the action step at the earliest opportunity.

REFLECT ON WHAT YOU NEED

STRETCH YOUR BODY

Be kind to your body by stretching it periodically, especially before and after exercise and if you tend to sit for long periods of time. See page 51 for tips on Moving Mindfully. When doing these movements, make sure both feet are flat on the floor so the body is balanced. You can do all of these stretches together or do different ones periodically through the day.

When doing any kind of stretching, make adjustments to take account of your own vulnerabilities—particularly when moving the neck—and always treat your body gently, exploring its boundaries rather than pushing through them mindlessly.

SHOULDERS

Sit up tall (see page 38). Become aware of your shoulders and as you breathe in, lift your shoulders up to your ears… as you breathe out, bring your shoulder blades together behind you so your chest opens up. Do this for at least 3–4 rounds.

Then reverse it to work the back instead. As you breathe in, lift the shoulders up to your ears… as you breathe out, bring the shoulders forward so the back opens up. Do this for at least 3–4 rounds.

ARMS

1. Stretch your left arm across your body at chest height. With the right arm, gently press the left arm into the body. Feel the stretch along the shoulder and arm and breathe into it. Notice if you start holding your breath and if you do, just remember to breathe! Repeat with the opposite arm.

2. Interlock your fingers and pushing your palms out, stretch out your arms in front of you and then move them above your head. Keeping your head upright and facing forward. Stretch upward and then release. Repeat.

3. As you breathe in, raise one arm up to the ceiling. As you breathe out, stretch that arm over your head to the opposite side in a side stretch. Keep the torso upright and breathe into the stretch for a few rounds. Breathe in as you bring the arm back upright, breathe out as you relax the shoulder and float the arm back down to your side. Repeat on the opposite side.

NECK

1. Imagine you have a blob of paint on the end of your nose and making small gentle circular movements, "paint" circles with your nose. Do this one way for several revolutions and then reverse. Keep the movements slow and steady; you can make the circles larger or smaller, as you wish.

2. Take your attention into your right ear. Just become aware of the right ear. Then slowly move the right ear in the general direction of the right shoulder. There is no expectation that the two will meet. If the right shoulder lifts to meet the right ear, just relax it down. Go as far as feels okay for you and then just rest there and imagine you are breathing in and out of the stretch in the neck. Then slowly bring the head back to center. Repeat on the other side. Keep all movements slow and gentle.

3. Finally, take your attention into your head and knowing it's the heaviest part of the body, gently begin moving the chin toward the chest. You may like to experiment with closing your eyes. Slowly moving the chin toward the chest, stretching out the back of the neck and stopping at whatever point feels far enough for you. Hang out there for a few breaths and then, gently moving in reverse, raise the head back upright to center.

LEGS AND FEET

Sit up tall. Stretch one leg out in front of you and move the ankle clockwise for a few rounds and then counterclockwise. Shake out the lower leg. Put that foot down and repeat on the other side.

HANDS AND FINGERS

Bring the fingers of one hand together and with the other hand, gently bend the fingers back slightly, stretching the wrist. Hold for a moment or two. Repeat. Then repeat on the opposite hand. Wiggle your fingers and shake out your hands.

TWIST AT THE WAIST

Sit up tall (see page 38) with both feet flat on the floor, keeping your feet and knees facing forward, then twist at the waist. When you've gone as far as feels okay for you, feel the stretch along the length of the torso and the neck and breathe into it. Slowly move back to face forward center and then do the other side. Do this a few times, moving slowly gently and letting your head move with your body.

WAKE UP AND ENERGIZE YOURSELF

I first came across this Tui'na self-massage as a qigong practice by Francesco Garripoli, but its origins are over 1,000 years old and it was developed by the monks of the Shaolin Temple in China. It uses the same principle as acupuncture and reflexology— releasing chi or energy that is trapped in the body.

You can do this self-care practice if you are feeling tired and sluggish. Usually you would do it standing up. However, you can choose to focus on different parts—for example, just work on the eyes if they are feeling tired—and remain seated.

Stand with your feet parallel and hip-width apart and your knees soft. Take a few moments to connect with the feet on the floor and have an awareness of the whole body. Begin to tune into your breathing.

Hold your hands in front of the belly as if you are holding a large beach ball. Begin to become aware of your hands—the palms of the hands, the fingers. Wherever you place your mind, your energy follows.

FACE

If you wear glasses, set them aside. Begin to rub your palms together quite briskly to generate some heat. After a few moments, place the palms flat on your face. Begin to gently "wash" your face, moving your fingers and palms across the landscape of the face. This stimulates the epidermal layer of skin.

SCALP

Using the tips of your fingers, start at the hairline and move your fingertips across and around the scalp. You can be reasonably vigorous as you stimulate the scalp— it has 17 key points where acupuncture meridians intersect and affect the entire body, so you are energizing the whole body.

EARS

With the right thumb and index finger, take hold of the right earlobe and then with the left thumb and index finger reach over the head and take hold of the top of the right ear. Carefully press along the profile of the ear and gently tug the ear (being careful of any jewelry). You are energizing blood flow. Repeat with the opposite side

EYES

Place your thumbs across the palms and fold the fingers over to make a fist. Starting between the eyes, draw the fists along and around the bony eye socket. Pressure can be firm when going around the eye socket, but ease off when stroking across the closed eyes. Repeat several times. The eyes are connected to the liver meridian. This is a good one to do any time to relieve tired eyes.

SINUS

Still with your hands in fists, come down from between the eyes down both sides of the nose and across the cheeks, opening the sinuses and stimulating the lungs.

JAW

Open the fists and using the fingertips, rub around the lips and the jaw. Move along both sides of the jaw right up into the TMJ—that dip behind the ear. As you rub the TMJ, close the mouth and breathe deeply. This area is related to the stomach meridian; stimulation energizes the stomach and releases tension, as well as keeping the skin healthy.

THROAT

Using the flat of the fingers, rub up and down the throat, continue into the jaw line. This stimulates the lymph nodes.

SHOULDERS AND ARMS

Making the hands into fists again, gently pound along the left shoulder and down the arms, patting both under and along the top. Then repeat on the other side.

LEGS

Using the flat of the hand with fingers pointing downward, pat down the chest toward the legs. Bend over and slap down the front of the thighs, the shin, and then down the back and both inner and outer sides. Repeat on the other leg. This is a great way to activate the blood flow, particularly if you have been sitting or standing for a long time.

KIDNEYS

Making your hands into fists again, gently pummel the lower back around the kidneys. This area is for lower back pain and stress.

TO FINISH

Relax the arms and legs and shake yourself out like a rag doll. Let your limbs go limp and relax as you bounce gently. Then swing the arms and move the body in a way that feels good for you.

Finally, with your hands positioned low at your waist, make tight fists and begin to throw the hands out, opening them as you do so. Repeat this action several times as you toss off the stagnant chi and energize the whole body. Kick each leg out and shake it. Really let go! Pause and notice how you feel.

MEDITATING KINDFULLY

Meditating (see page 35) gives us the opportunity to be with all the different mind states and also to practice relating to them in a different way. Although kindness is implicit within the attitudes we cultivate (see page 26), we can make it more explicit by setting an intention to cultivate compassion and kindness rather than self-criticism during our practice.

When you meditate, are you practicing kindness or self-criticism and self-judgment? Do you notice thoughts around "*I should have sat for longer,*" or perhaps "*I should be able to stop my mind wandering,*" or "*I shouldn't be so restless*"—the list goes on! The word "should" is a red flag that tells us we are judging ourselves against some imaginary yardstick.

TRY THIS

When you meditate, take the time to settle into your seat (see page 38) and find a position that is alert yet relaxed.

Then, consciously set an intention to practice self-kindness in this sitting.

At any time during the meditation when you notice self-criticism or judgments arising around your experience, notice and acknowledge them. Tune into how it feels in the head, heart, and body.

Remind yourself it's okay—minds wander, limbs get restless. This is your experience right now.

Remind yourself that there is no need to strive toward a particular experience. What is interesting is what is happening right now… and practicing being kind and non-judgmental toward that.

Try it…

REFLECT ON YOUR MEDITATION

_____

_____

_____

_____

_____

_____

_____

_____

_____

_____

_____

_____

_____

_____

_____

_____

_____

_____

_____

_____

Week 34

HOW DO YOU MOTIVATE YOURSELF?

Do you motivate yourself through kindness, support, and encouragement, or through shame and fear? Although we often think that self-criticism can be a powerful motivator, in fact it is the opposite. Motivating yourself through love and kindness is far more powerful than doing so through fear.

Motivation through self-criticism is associated with reduced performance and increased levels of rumination and procrastination, as well as poor mental health. Self-critics tend to approach goals motivated by fear of avoiding failure and disapproval—that is, a sense of threat—rather than a sense of interest and curiosity. When we operate from a sense of threat, our thinking is narrower and less creative.

In contrast, when we practice self-compassion we are less afraid of failing and when we do fail, we are more likely to try again and we are more motivated to try to learn from past mistakes.

Sometimes people are afraid that being self-compassionate means they can't be ambitious or push themselves to do better. However, the key is how you motivate yourself. Self-compassion motivates like a good coach, acknowledging mistakes or things that you could do differently, and encouraging with kindness and support rather than with blame and self-criticism and stories of "not being good enough." Which way would you prefer to be motivated?

Week 34

TRY THIS

Do this reflection over a period of time and use the prompts below to reflect on what you notice as you do this practice.

1. Is there a personal trait you criticize yourself for because you think that will help motivate you to change? It could be that you are quick to get angry, or you think you are overweight, or you don't stand up for yourself enough… Choose one and write it in your journal or on the page overleaf.

2. Over a period of time, notice how the self-criticism makes you feel. As long as it feels okay, tune into the emotional pain that your self-criticism causes. Write down how it makes you feel emotionally, along with any physical sensations you become aware of. Give yourself compassion, warmth, and kindness for the experience of feeling so judged.

You can't do anything differently until you acknowledge how things really are. Noticing and acknowledging this forms the mindfulness element of self-compassion (see page 12).

REFLECT ON HOW YOU MOTIVATE YOURSELF

MOTIVATE YOURSELF THROUGH SELF-COMPASSION

In Week 34, we looked at how you motivate yourself. Once you become aware of *how* you do so and connect with how that makes you feel physically and how it affects your mood, you can begin to experiment with motivating yourself in a different way—with kindness.

Is there a kinder way you could motivate yourself to make change if it is needed? How would someone who cared about you motivate you?

A good coach might point out the unhelpful behavior you were engaging in, but at the same time would encourage you to do something different in a positive way. What words would they use? Be specific…write them down if that is helpful. Learn them by heart so you can easily bring them to mind when you need to.

Every time you catch yourself being judgmental about your unwanted trait (see page 143), notice the pain of that judgment—how it feels physically in the body as well as emotionally—and offer yourself compassion. Remind yourself of those encouraging words and phrases and say them to yourself. Practice changing the way you talk to yourself so it is more encouraging and supportive. It may feel strange at first, but keep practicing!

Here are some examples of how unhelpful phrases might be rephrased to be more compassionate:

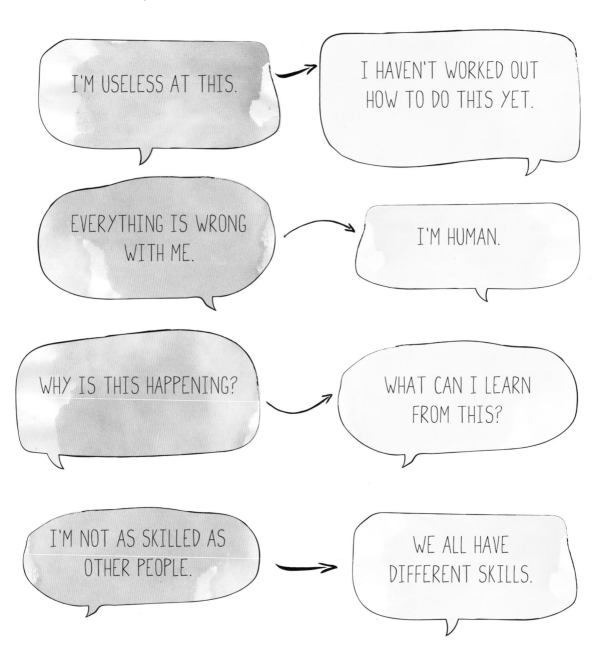

Week 35

Write down the typical unhelpful phrases that you often use and then rewrite them
from a self-compassionate point of view. Practice saying the latter and notice how the
different words affect you.

UNHELPFUL PHRASE

REPHRASED WITH SELF-COMPASSION

_____

_____

_____

_____

_____

_____

_____

_____

_____

_____

_____

_____

_____

_____

JUST BEING

Are you someone who is always busy and on the go? How often do you give yourself the gift of time—the time just to pause without any agenda and simply create some space for yourself.

Taking a moment and intentionally being still, allowing ourselves to be with whatever is present is a simple practice we can do any time, anywhere, for any length of time. How do we do this? The easiest way is to let go of trying to do anything in particular and allow things to be exactly as they are. It's the opposite of "doing," which most of us are experts at!

There are no instructions for posture; you can sit, stand, or lie down in any position that feels comfortable. If that means softening into an armchair or on to a bed, then do that. Weather permitting, you might like to lie on the grass looking up at the sky or you may prefer to meander around. Notice what you are drawn to.

You may become aware of a tightening or tensing. If the body relaxes when you become aware of this, then that's okay. If the tension remains, that's okay. There's no need to force anything. Just allow the body to be as it is from moment to moment.

This is a practice in just being as you are. There are no instructions to focus on the breath or the body; no need to notice your thoughts or what you are feeling. If your mind wanders and you feel like seeing where it goes, then follow it. There is no agenda. There is no wrong way to do this. Just be exactly as you are for as short or as long as you wish.

Afterward, you might want to reflect on how it feels when you are not being busy? Check in with the head, heart, and body. You may find it physically uncomfortable or perhaps you feel guilty. Just acknowledge whatever arises. The tyranny of the to-do list can be challenging to shake off!

REFLECT ON JUST BEING

WHAT NOURISHES YOU DAILY?

Choosing what we do and how we do it is one way we can practice kindness to ourselves and others. This exercise is an opportunity for you to reflect on what you do every day.

Choose a day that most typically reflects your lifestyle at the moment. It may be at work or at home. Make a list of everything you do from the moment you get up until you go to bed. Be as specific as you can and break down larger activities into smaller chunks, if possible.

PART I

Go back over your list and grade each activity with a "+" or "–", depending on whether you think it is something that nourishes you or something that drains you.

Notice if you hesitate over some activities and what comes up around that hesitation. If an activity could be either—it is neutral—mark it with a "/". What makes something tip from being okay to not okay?

Once you have completed your list, take a moment to read back through it. What do you notice? Are there any surprises? Jot down some notes of what comes up for you.

You may notice that an activity's rating depends on whom you are doing it with, or perhaps how you are feeling physically, mentally, and emotionally. If you are feeling stressed or under the weather, you are more likely to struggle with more difficult situations.

PART 2

Go back over your list and reflect on any activities that are neutral (/) or draining (−). What would it take to make those activities less depleting or even become nourishing?

If it feels too much to make a draining activity nourishing, reflect on whether there is anything you could do either before, after, or during to make it neutral?

For example, if you have a regular stressful meeting at work, make sure you are in the best shape for it by preparing thoroughly for it in advance. In the meeting, ground yourself by using the touch points of the body with the chair or a hot/cold drink, tuning into the breath for a round or two. After the meeting. perhaps take a walk outside to clear your head or talk to a supportive friend or co-worker.

Try to come up with as many ideas as you can. By doing this you are taking care of yourself and offering yourself kindness and care in a difficult situation, rather than trying to make the uncomfortable feelings go away.

Sometimes we may indulge in an activity by choice that actually makes us feel worse—for example, going on social media or watching the news. You may be keen to keep up with what is going on, but find that the constant exposure feeds your

Week 37

anxiety. Once you notice, you could give yourself a break or set some boundaries so, for example, only check in with social media or the news once a day for a limited time.

Now consider if there is anything you can do to transform a neutral activity into one that is more nourishing. The attitude you bring to an activity can be significant; one of curiosity and interest (even if you don't like it) is going to feel more nourishing than one of irritation or boredom. Let's look at eating as an example: multi-tasking by eating at your desk or eating on the go without any awareness can be transformed by simply paying attention to the sensory experience of eating—even if it's just for that first mouthful. Be as creative as you can.

So-called wasted moments in your day, when perhaps you are waiting for other people to do something or waiting for someone to arrive, can become more nourishing by being used as opportunities for a moment or two of practice—breathing through the feet in the floor perhaps or simply checking in with yourself and acknowledging how you are doing.

Write your ideas down and choose one to implement at a time. Don't try to do more than that at once, otherwise you will feel overwhelmed and be more likely to give up.

REFLECT ON WHAT NOURISHES YOU

_____

_____

_____

_____

_____

_____

_____

_____

_____

_____

_____

_____

_____

_____

_____

_____

_____

_____

_____

CONNECTING WITH STRANGERS

Most of the people in our lives are strangers. We may see them regularly, we may know their first name but not their surname. We often label them by the job they do— the waitress, the nurse, the security guard. We neither like or dislike them, but we are not invested in them emotionally. Because of this we often switch off from them—we don't engage with them or see them as individuals—we may not even notice them.

This neutral attitude can easily tip into negativity when they don't act in the way we want them to—we may get frustrated if they are serving us slowly, for example.

In the traditional Buddhist Loving Kindness meditation, there is a stage where you actively bring to mind and cultivate kindness and caring for someone who you regard as neutral. You can also do this as an informal practice as here. It isn't about changing anyone else—it is about cultivating a connection between you and the people who inhabit your life.

TRY THIS

You can experiment with any of the following:

* Make eye contact with anyone who serves you.
* Choose one neutral person and make an intention to greet them warmly every time you see them. If you know their name, use it. Do this regularly.
* Choose one neutral person and when you come across them silently offer them words of kindness. Some suggestions might be "May you be happy;" "May you be well;" "May you experience kindness in your life." Do this regularly.
* Smile.
* Choose one neutral person in your life and reflect on what you have in common. It may be physical attributes, colors you wear, what you like to eat or drink… How many things do you share in common?

REFLECT ON CONNECTING WITH STRANGERS

_____

_____

_____

_____

_____

_____

_____

_____

_____

_____

_____

_____

_____

_____

ENJOY WHAT YOU EAT

Eating well is one of the easiest ways we can offer kindness to the body, but it is also one of the easiest to forget. When we are busy or ravenous, we might grab fast food on the go or when we are feeling down or stressed we might "treat ourselves" to something loaded with empty calories, which then temporarily raises blood sugar before impacting negatively on our mood. Even if we do prepare a healthy meal, we often eat it while focusing on a multitude of things other than smell, taste, and texture.

STEP 1

Take some time to notice your eating patterns. What do you eat regularly? How does your eating pattern change when you are feeling stressed or down? What links do you notice between what you eat, how much you eat, and how you feel physically and mentally in terms of energy and mood? Do you notice any impact on your skin, hair, and nails? Make eating the object of your attention, but in the spirit of kindness rather than condemnation. This is about gathering feedback, so don't give yourself a hard time if what you notice isn't how you would like it to be.

Changes in eating patterns can be a really helpful red flag, highlighting how you are feeling physically and mentally. If you are sleep deprived, for example, you will most likely have an increased appetite and make more unhealthy choices due to the disruption to the body's regulation system, including the hormones responsible for suppressing and stimulating appetite. If you are tuned in and notice a pattern, you can take early action to look after yourself and make better food choices.

Week 39

STEP 2

Experiment with being present while you are eating. Pay attention to the scents, sounds, textures, and taste of each mouthful, or at the very least the first bite you take. What do you notice?

Often the experience feels richer and, because you are noticing it, you will remember it, so it becomes a nourishing experience (assuming what you are eating is good!). Savoring the experience means you will naturally eat more slowly, so you will have time to pick up the body's physical cues when you are full, which means you are less likely to overeat.

Does this mean you can never have a sweet treat? Absolutely not. But being honest with yourself about what you are eating and its impact on you will mean it will be just that—a treat rather than the norm. When you are enjoying a treat, savor and enjoy it, rather than judging yourself for having it.

Look for the middle way between being overly rigid or overly lax about what you eat and remember that what you eat is fueling your body and your mind.

There is evidence to suggest that people who practice self-compassion are more likely to make healthier choices.

LISTENING DEEPLY

Sometimes listening in silence is the greatest kindness you can give to someone. Much of the time when we are with others, although we may be present physically, our mind and our attention is somewhere else. We half-listen, jump in with "me too" stories, or simply tune out. We often don't even realize that we are doing it or are unaware of how much both parties are missing by not being present.

Begin by noticing your habitual patterns when in conversation with others. Just notice with kindly awareness and without self-criticism or blame.

- Are you present much of the time or is your attention somewhere else?
- What is pulling your attention away?
- Who do you regularly tune out from?
- Do you regularly interrupt others?
- Are you shutting them down, telling them what to do or think or feel?

When you are talking to someone else and their attention is elsewhere, how does that impact on you? When someone jumps in and tells you what to do to solve your problem without being asked, how do you feel? How about the opposite? What is it like when someone deeply listens to you?

Become familiar with both states. Which one do you prefer? Offer to others what you would like to receive. Give them your full attention. Listening deeply means being present in mind as well as body. Receiving what is being said without jumping in to fix or give advice unless specifically requested. When you give someone your attention, you notice more than the words that are being said. You hear the nuances in tone and pick up on subtle changes in body language.

TRY THIS

It can be helpful to make an intention to be present with one specific person—a child or family member, perhaps.

Keep reminding yourself of your intention. Regularly tune into the touch points of the body and notice how it feels physically in the body when you become aware of the impulse to jump in, interrupt, or fix.

It will take time to learn to respond differently, so practice patience and don't give yourself a hard time when you forget. Every time you are present, you will both experience a benefit. Notice those benefits and acknowledge them in order to motivate yourself to keep going. Listening deeply will impact positively on you and the people you are listening to.

SPEAKING WITH KINDNESS

You can cultivate kindness in speech in different ways, including becoming aware of your motivation. Your motivation feeds your intention, which in turn underlies any action you take, including the words you use and how you utter them, as well as your whole demeanor and body language. Kindness is characterized by openness and warmth, rather than threat and anger.

Practicing speaking with kindness is particularly helpful with difficult conversations whether at work or with family members. Are you trying to score points or hurt someone, or are you trying to find a compromise or a way through a conflict? Even if the message you are delivering is unwelcome, you can still give it with kindness, support, and respect.

TRY THIS

Try to avoid having a difficult conversation when emotions are running high or if you are feeling stressed. Go for a brisk walk outside, if possible, to get a change of perspective.

Before a difficult conversation, take a moment to pause, connect with the touch points of the body, and tune into your breathing. Remind yourself of what is motivating you—this will depend on the context, but it might be love, warmth, respect, caring. Hold an image of the person you are about to speak to in your heart and remind yourself of how you would like them to feel during and after your conversation.

You may want to repeat loving kindness phrases such as "May I be kind to others" or "May I speak with kindness and respect" or "May I speak from the heart."

When speaking, periodically touch in to your own experience. You are still present with the person you are speaking with, but you are also aware of your own body, emotions, and thoughts, noticing the thought story and holding that with compassion.

If you feel strong emotions arising, connect with the touch points of the body and imagine you are breathing through your feet on the floor. It's always fine to pause.

If you can connect with your heart and your wish to support and be kind and caring to another person, this will come through in your communication.

REFLECT ON YOUR CONVERSATION

_____

_____

_____

_____

_____

_____

_____

_____

_____

_____

_____

_____

_____

_____

_____

_____

LEARNING KINDNESS FROM OTHERS

Everyone interprets kindness in their own way and we can learn a lot by observing how others practice kindness to themselves and other people, and the many forms that kindness can take.

Make an intention to notice and observe how others practice kindness in its widest possible sense. Observe in as many different environments as possible: at home, at work, when you are out and about; as well as kindness to people, animals, pets, the environment. Be inspired by people you hear about in the media, or from friends and family. Are there ways you can give back to your community by offering your time or help supporting others?

An example that springs to mind for me is when our elderly neighbor bought a new washing machine, but lost the instruction booklet. Unable to make sense of the high-spec touchpad or go online to search for help, she became frustrated and annoyed with herself as well everyone else! Hearing about what had happened, my husband found the correct instruction booklet online, downloaded and printed it, and then spent an hour showing our neighbor how to use her machine. This was a practical interpretation of kindness to others.

TRY THIS

Just notice and record any ideas that particularly inspire you. Choose one at a time to experiment with. Offer kindness without any expectation of receiving anything in return. Be sensitive of others and take care not to impose "kindness" on them.

Let go of any expectations about how you think it should make you feel and instead simply tune into the head, heart, and body both at the time of doing it and when you reflect afterward.

What do you notice?

REFLECT ON HOW OTHERS ARE KIND

_____
_____
_____
_____
_____
_____
_____
_____
_____
_____
_____
_____
_____
_____
_____
_____
_____
_____
_____
_____
_____

THROUGH THE EYES OF A FRIEND

When we think of offering the qualities of kindness such as caring, love, gentleness, warmth, compassion, and tenderness to others it seems an obvious thing to do, and something we can easily relate to. However, sometimes offering these positive emotions to ourselves can feel quite different—almost selfish at times. Practicing self-kindness is anything but selfish, but you can help yourself overcome this potential obstacle by removing "I" and "me" from the equation.

TRY THIS

First of all think of a time when a friend or family member was struggling. It doesn't matter why they were finding things tough, but bring to mind how they felt and how you responded to those feelings. What did you say? Can you remember the words or phrases you used? What tone of voice did you use? How did you behave? Did you do anything specific? Write down what you can remember.

Now bring to mind a difficult situation you are facing. As you do so, connect with any touch points of the body and the surface supporting you. Tune into your breathing. Visualize yourself if that's possible for you.

Addressing yourself by your name and in the third person, talk to yourself as if you were talking to your friend when they were struggling. Use the same words and phrases and offer them in the same tone of voice.

Acknowledge the situation and how it is making you feel; acknowledge if there are things that you've messed up or could have done differently, and support and encourage yourself in the same way you would a friend in need. Coach yourself rather than beating yourself up.

Afterward, reflect on what you notice, how you are feeling now, and how this was different if at all to the way you would normally behave toward yourself when you are struggling.

You can always do this as a writing practice—the instructions remain the same, but instead write a letter to yourself in the third person. Why not physically write it and post it to yourself?

REFLECT ON SELF-KINDNESS

_____

_____

_____

_____

_____

_____

_____

_____

_____

_____

_____

_____

_____

WHEN YOU STRUGGLE WITH PEOPLE YOU LOVE

It's not always easy to show kindness to those we love. Many of us will struggle at times with challenging family situations. Perhaps you are taking care of an elderly parent or other relative, or coping with a challenging teenager or toddler. Despite loving someone, you may still feel conflicting negative emotions such as anger, impatience, resentment, and then associated self-blame (or blaming others), guilt and judgment for feeling that way. It becomes a vicious circle and it's common to feel stuck and as if nothing is ever going to change.

The first step is always to acknowledge how you are feeling. Pretending everything is okay is simply denial and those negative emotions will manifest in another way. It can be really hard to admit you are having these thoughts and experiencing these negative emotions, but it is an important first step toward accepting your experience.

The following scenario is with an elderly parent, but it could be adapted for any interaction when you are struggling with someone.

BEFORE YOU MEET OR PHONE YOUR PARENT

Acknowledge how you feel by checking in with your head, heart, and body. Notice whatever is present and name it. "Resentment is here," for example. Tune into your breathing for a round or two. You can remind yourself how much you love your parent, despite finding the current situation challenging. You can remind yourself of any suffering or difficulties he or she may be experiencing currently and offer some words of loving kindness (see page 63). Mentally connect with all the other people in the world who are currently experiencing something similar. Challenges in family relationships is a universal experience.

Week 44

DURING THE VISIT OR CONVERSATION

Be present. Ground yourself by noticing the touch points of the body with any surfaces such as your feet on the floor, being in contact with a seat, or holding a hot drink. Tune into your breath periodically. Silently offer your parent and/or yourself words of loving kindness. Remind yourself of why you love him or her despite the current situation. Be as specific as you can.

AFTER THE VISIT OR CONVERSATION

Do another check-in with the head, heart, and body. Acknowledge how you are feeling now. Ground yourself in the breath and body. Ask yourself "What do I need right now?" Give yourself some care and kindness, whether that is taking care of yourself physically or mentally. Try to choose specific activities that are easy to implement with little planning and then do them.

When faced with the challenge of sick or elderly parents, there is little you can do about the situation, but you can influence your own response to it and intentionally practice kindness toward yourself—and them.

When you notice thoughts of resentment, guilt, or blame, don't ignore them or give yourself a hard time about them. Remind yourself you are doing your best in a difficult situation and of how much you love them regardless of how the situation makes you feel.

PROCESSING YOUR EXPERIENCE WITH SELF-COMPASSION

As you will have been discovering, there are many different ways to cultivate kindness toward yourself. This practice is about intentionally cultivating self-compassion in your daily life when you experience strong negative emotions. It was developed as part of the MSC program (see page 7) and, although it is designed to be a journal activity (writing things down often gives us perspective and helps us connect with how we feel at a deeper level than our thinking mind), you can do it as a reflection.

Whether you are writing it down or reflecting internally, it is helpful to have a note of the three stages of reflection to keep you on track. Ideally you would do this daily for a week or so.

TRY THIS

Each evening reflect back on your day and bring to mind anything that you feel bad about—perhaps you experienced physical or psychological pain, snapped at someone, or the way you behaved fell short of what you hoped for, and so you judge yourself harshly. Then systematically draw on the three components of self-compassion—mindfulness, common humanity, and kindness (see page 12)—to process the experience step by step.

STEP 1: Mindfulness—see the experience as it is and notice how it made you feel. For example, "I felt frustrated and then I got angry with the person serving me for not going fast enough. Afterward I felt annoyed with myself as it was my fault I was late because I pressed snooze." Describe it factually without any added drama. If you noticed how it made you feel physically, you can always acknowledge that too.

STEP 2: Common humanity—remind yourself of the bigger picture. Perhaps, "I often snap at others when I am stressed. Most people do. No one is perfect." Acknowledge the context for your reaction: "I pressed snooze because I'm feeling exhausted because of work/the baby."

STEP 3: Kindness—offer yourself some words of support and kindness. Perhaps "It's okay. You are exhausted. You didn't mean it. Remember this and behave differently next time. We are all a work in progress." You might ask yourself, "What do I need right now? How can I take care of myself?"

Doing this regularly over a period of time will help you process the everyday struggles we all face in a healthier, kinder way. Reflecting in a systematic way will help embed the three stages in your mind, so it starts becoming second nature to process your experience with self-compassion rather than criticism.

REFLECT

_____

_____

_____

_____

_____

_____

_____

_____

CONNECTING WITH HEART

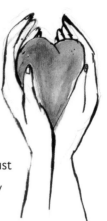

How do you connect with your friends? Are you someone who remembers their birthday or the anniversary of their parent's passing? Do you remember to ask about a problem they were having at work or with their child the last time you talked? Do you phone them rather than just hitting the "sad face" emoji on a social media post? Do you ask them how they are and really listen to their answer?

Technology allows us to connect more easily but less meaningfully with those we care about. Instead of having a small circle of close friends, we are more likely to have a wide circle of acquaintances and interact with everyone more superficially.

THINGS TO REFLECT ON

How we relate to others matters and regardless of what we have been guilty of in the past, there is always an opportunity to begin anew.

- How often do you connect with the people who matter to you? When you do, are you present or distracted? Do you show up for them at difficult times?
- What does connecting with heart mean to you? It may mean different things for specific people. Reflect on this and make a note to help you remember.
- What do you do that brings joy, happiness, support to the people around you?
- Notice all the positive ways you already connect with heart and make an intention to do more of them.
- Notice positive ways other people connect with you that you appreciate and try them out with others if appropriate. However, don't assume that what you like/find helpful is going to be the same for everyone else.
- What makes the people you care about happy or what supports them? Can you contribute to that? Practice being thoughtful of others.

How you are can make a difference to others. Stay connected with your heart. Keep it genuine. Give without expectation of return.

REFLECT ON HOW YOU CONNECT

A ROOM WITH A VIEW

What do you see when you look out of your windows? Is the outside area clean and tidy? Are there plants and flowers? You may not be able to control how your neighborhood looks, but you can make choices about your home environment and influence how it looks. If you are really busy, it can feel like just another thing to do and a low priority one at that, but investing some effort in improving what you see out of your window will feed your soul.

TRY THIS

If you have a garden or outside space, make an intention to look after it. You can do this gradually, spending a bit of time each week outside weeding and tidying up and planting flowers. Plant bulbs or seeds with a view to the long game—you'll enjoy them in the months to come. If you don't have an outside space, you can still bring nature to you. Plant a window box or have pots of herbs in the kitchen, add color with fresh flowers and house plants.

You can suspend a bird feeder from any window and encourage visitors by making sure it's always topped up with food and fresh water. Taking care of birds and plants is another way of spreading some kindness—and it will lift your spirits too.

Take some time to survey your home—look outside your front door, out of different windows, review any outdoor space, what could you do to improve its aspect? Make a list of any ideas you have. You don't need to do them all at once. Writing them down will help you remember your intention.

HOW DO YOU TAKE CARE OF YOURSELF WHEN YOU ARE STRESSED?

Experiencing difficult periods comes with the territory of being human. At these times, the body's stress reaction is activated and it moves into survival mode. This is one of the body's most primitive and essential systems—the one that helps keep us alive in times of danger. When faced with life and death, there is no time to practice kindness. Thankfully, the body's stress reaction is more likely to be activated by something that is annoying, yes, frustrating for sure, but not life-threatening, such as your computer crashing or being stuck in roadworks or forgetting an appointment. These are the moments when it is important to practice kindness and compassion.

NOTICE YOUR TRIGGERS

Take a moment to reflect on what makes you stressed. Keep it real by focusing on the immediate period. Make a list of what has stressed you out in the last week or two. What was it about these situations that made you feel stressed? What was the story playing out in your head? We often feel stressed when things are out of our control. We may move into unhelpful patterns of thinking such as catastrophizing or over-generalizing that "these things always happen to me."

Become familiar with your own stress signature. Notice how it feels in the body, how it affects your behavior. Notice what type of situations are more likely to affect you negatively. When you observe something in this way, you are already somewhat removed from it—you've gained perspective. This distance gives you the opportunity to do something different.

Overleaf are some ideas of things you can do that will bring you into the moment, rather than getting swept away by "what ifs" of the future or "shoulds" of the past. None of these things will make a difficult situation disappear, but they can help you be with any negative emotions that might be arising.

Week 48

Simply preventing things escalating into overwhelm can be helpful.

TRY THIS

- Notice if you are holding your breath and, if so, let it go and take a deep breath in
- Imagine you are breathing through the soles of the feet
- Take a walk indoors or out
- Look out of a window
- Talk to someone
- Remind yourself that some things are outside of your control
- Acknowledge how you are feeling—name the monster, such as "Anxiety is here" and don't give yourself a hard time for feeling this way
- Connect with any touch points of the body in contact with the ground or other surface like a seat, wall, steering wheel of the car, etc
- Give yourself a hug—hold your arms across the body and exert some pressure
- Hold a hot/cold drink between your hands and just tune into those sensations

Once you have a sense of the type of thing you find helpful, practice it whenever difficult moments arise. If you can also practice doing it when things are okay, you will be able to recall it more readily.

REFLECT ON HOW YOU DEAL WITH STRESS

ENJOYING THE STRAWBERRY MOMENTS

There are times when you may experience longer periods of stress, perhaps work-related or due to illness, or perhaps it's down to a relationship breakdown or bereavement. Even positive occasions like getting married or becoming a parent can make you feel stressed. How can you practice self-kindness in these situations?

There is a teaching story about a woman being chased by tigers: she's running and running, but suddenly comes to a cliff edge. She begins to climb down but slips and is only saved from falling by grabbing hold of a vine, but there's a mouse gnawing at the vine, so the vine is getting thinner and thinner. She's hanging on for her life, with tigers above and below. She suddenly sees a wild strawberry just within her reach. She takes the strawberry, places it in her mouth, and thoroughly enjoys it.

When it feels as if our life is falling apart, we can forget to notice and enjoy the "strawberry moments." These are always available to us if we are willing to look; they may be quite fleeting—a momentary tuning into the present moment and acknowledging something pleasant. They don't have to be five-star experiences.

CULTIVATING KINDNESS

It's important to acknowledge how you are actually feeling—that you are experiencing a difficult period in your life right now—and intentionally cultivating some kindness and helping the body regain some balance. Always remember that it's important to take action without any expectations. Some suggestions:

- Scheduling an activity that will nourish you physically, mentally, or spiritually
- Take some exercise that will raise the heart rate and help the body release pent-up stress hormones
- Do an activity that you might not particularly enjoy, but one that gives you a sense of satisfaction or control—cleaning and decluttering are always good ones!
- Enlist the help of family and friends to support you. This might include giving you some time for yourself or help with chores to share the burden.

SHARING THE PAIN OF OTHERS

When people we care about are experiencing a challenging situation, it can be hard to know how to respond. We want to help, but often there is nothing we can do or say to make things better. This practice is an informal way of offering kindness, love, caring (whatever positive qualities are appropriate) in these type of situations. You can do it any time, anywhere, and without anyone knowing you are doing it.

TRY THIS

When you breathe in, you are breathing in a willingness to embrace and share the pain the person is experiencing. When you breathe out, you are letting go and relaxing. It's a continuous touching into the pain and then letting it go—in tune with your breathing. So when you are faced with someone who is experiencing difficulties, imagine you are breathing in the difficulty (name it, such as "pain") and breathing out a positive quality of your choice (such as "love/peace/calm").

It may seem counterintuitive to intentionally breathe in the difficulty, but you are only holding it briefly before letting it go. However, if it feels too challenging keep it abstract by breathing in the dark (blackness) and breathing out light (white). This practice is about connecting to suffering and joy, both of which are intrinsic to being human. Instead of avoiding suffering in the way we habitually do, we practice connecting with it and acknowledging it as part and parcel of life and interconnected with joy and all the positive qualities of life. Buddhist teacher and author Pema Chodron describes it as being willing to share the pain of others on the in-breath and pleasure, delight, love on the out-breath.

You can do this practice for yourself as well as doing it as a way of cultivating kindness and other positive qualities for other people.

COUNT THE WAYS TO BE KIND

We often don't take the time to notice the many ways we can practice self-kindness.
Begin to notice what nourishes you—what makes
you feel better.

Jot the ideas down here. Keep adding to the list and begin to intentionally
incorporate the suggestions into your everyday life. Pay attention to the
simple things that give small pleasures. These are often easier to do than
5-star activities that often take planning and money.

1. _____

2. _____

3. _____

4. _____

5. _____

6. _____

7. _____

8. _____

9. _____

10. _____

ALLOW MYSELF TO SAY NO
SLOW DOWN
ACKNOWLEDGE WHAT I DO WELL
HAVE A COMPUTER-FREE DAY
SIT IN THE SUN WITH A BOOK
LISTEN TO MY HEART
BUY SOME FRESH FLOWERS
APPRECIATE MY ACHIEVEMENTS
ENCOURAGE MYSELF

REFLECT

_____
_____
_____
_____
_____
_____
_____
_____
_____
_____

REFLECTING BACK AND LOOKING FORWARD

As your year of living kindfully ends, this is an opportunity to reflect back on what you have noticed and make some intentions about what you would like to take forward. What does living kindfully mean to you now? You can explore this in a reflective meditation and/or writing practice.

REFLECTIVE MEDITATION

Come to sit and take a few moments to tune into the touch points of the body and the breath. When you are ready, silently ask yourself, "What does living kindfully mean to me?" Let the question drop into your subconscious without any expectations of a particular answer. After a pause, repeat. Notice any ripples—a felt sense, words or phrases, or images. Just receive whatever arises. Continue repeating the question and then change the question to "What do I want to take away?" Repeat as before. You can substitute alternative questions or make up your own: What does kindness mean to me? What does self kindness mean to me? What does a life of kindness mean to me?

When you finish, pause for a moment and then, if you'd like to, make a note of anything that came up for you.

WRITING PRACTICE

- Set a timer for 5 minutes and have plenty of paper. Begin each sentence with the statement: *Living kindfully means*…. Don't edit, cross out, or stop writing.
- You can have some additional statements to weave in such as: *Kindness is*…; *Self-kindness is*… or make up some of your own.
- When the timer goes, stop writing and pause before reading your words. Notice as you do what arises for you—are there any surprises?

Pull out key words or phrases and write a short summary that completes the following: *Living Kindfully means that I will*…..

REFLECTIONS

_____

_____

_____

_____

_____

_____

_____

_____

_____

_____

_____

_____

_____

_____

_____

_____

_____

_____

_____

_____

_____

FURTHER REFLECTIONS

CHECKLIST OF ACTIVITIES

Mark off activities as you've completed them, and perhaps make a note of those
that particularly helped you.

☐ Week 1 _____

☐ Week 2 _____

☐ Week 3 _____

☐ Week 4 _____

☐ Week 5 _____

☐ Week 6 _____

☐ Week 7 _____

☐ Week 8 _____

☐ Week 9 _____

☐ Week 10 _____

☐ Week 11 _____

☐ Week 12 _____

☐ Week 13 _____

☐ Week 14 _____

☐ Week 15 _____

☐ Week 16 _____

☐ Week 17 _____

☐ Week 18 _____

☐ Week 19 _____

☐ Week 20 _____

☐ Week 21 _____

☐ Week 22 _____

☐ Week 23 _____

☐ Week 24 _____

☐ Week 25 _____

☐ Week 26 _____

☐ Week 27 _____

☐ Week 28 _____

☐ Week 29 _____

☐ Week 30 _____

☐ Week 31 _____

☐ Week 32 _____

☐ Week 33 _____

☐ Week 34 _____

☐ Week 35 _____

☐ Week 36 _____

☐ Week 37 _____

☐ Week 38 _____

☐ Week 39 _____

☐ Week 40 _____

☐ Week 41 _____

☐ Week 42 _____

☐ Week 43 _____

☐ Week 44 _____

☐ Week 45 _____

☐ Week 46 _____

☐ Week 47 _____

☐ Week 48 _____

☐ Week 49 _____

☐ Week 50 _____

☐ Week 51 _____

☐ Week 52 _____

RESOURCES

There are many books on mindfulness and compassion; however, authors and teachers I particularly find helpful around kindness and compassion include Sharon Salzberg, Pema Chodron, Christopher Germer, Kristin Neff, Erik van den Brink and Frits Koster, Jon Kabat-Zinn, and Tara Brach.

GUIDED MEDITATIONS

It can be helpful to meditate with guidance, particularly when you are starting out. Many of the authors listed above have guided practices available either through their websites or through digital publishers such as Sounds True (www.soundstrue.com). There are free guided practices to download at the following sites and include a mix of mindfulness, loving kindness, and self-compassion practices:

Center for Mindful Self-Compassion
https://centerformsc.org/practice-msc/guided-meditations-and-exercises/

Christopher Germer
https://chrisgermer.com/meditations/

Kristin Neff
https://self-compassion.org/category/exercises/guided-meditations

Centre for Mindfulness Research and Practice, North Wales
https://www.bangor.ac.uk/mindfulness/audio/index.php.en

FURTHER READING

Bartley, Trish *A Kindly Approach to Being with Cancer* (Wiley-Blackwell, 2016)

Burch, Vidymala *Living Well with Pain and Illness: Using Mindfulness to Free Yourself from Suffering* (Piatkus, 2008)

Chaskaslon, Michael *Mindfulness in Eight Weeks: The revolutionary 8-week plan to clear your mind and calm your life* (Harper Thorsons, 2014)

Germer, Christopher *The Mindful Path to Self-Compassion* (Guilford Press, 2009)

Kabat-Zinn, Jon *Wherever You Go, There You Are: Mindfulness Meditation for Everyday Life* (Piatkus, 2004)

Lehrhaupt, Linda and Meibert, Petra *Mindfulness-based Stress Reduction: the MBSR Program for Enhancing Health and Vitality* (New World Library, 2017

Neff, Kristin *Self-Compassion* (Yellow Kite, 2011)

Neff, Kristin and Germer, Christopher *The Mindful Self-Compassion Workbook: A Proven Way to Accept Yourself, Build Inner Strength, and Thrive* (Guilford Press, 2018)

Van den Brink, Erik, Koster, Frits *Mindfulness-Based Compassionate Living: A new training programme to deepen mindfulness with heartfulness* (Routledge, 2015)

Van den Brink, Erik, Koster, Frits, and Norton, Victoria *A Practical Guide to Mindfulness-Based Compassionate Living* (Routledge, 2018)

Williams, Mark, Teasdale, John, Segal, Zindel, and Kabat-Zinn, Jon *The Mindful Way through Depression: freeing yourself from Chronic Unhappiness* (Guilford Press, 2007)

INDEX

ACKNOWLEDGMENTS

I feel lucky and privileged to have been supported in my practice at different times by a host of wonderful teachers—some, like Melissa Blacker and David Rynick in person, but many others like Jack Kornfield, Pema Chodron, Sharon Salzberg, Christopher Germer, and Kristin Neff, to name just a few, only through their writings, but thanks and huge appreciation are due to all of them, as well as to my students who are always teaching me. Thanks too are due to those family and friends who always support me—in particular, Julia Bundgaard, Catherine Grey, Philippa Nuttall, and Rosemarie Paul.

Thanks too to the wonderful team at CICO Books: Cindy Richards for asking me in the first place, Dawn Bates for editing, Eliana Holder for designing, and Amy-Louise-Evans for the wonderful illustrations, plus all the other behind-the-scenes people in sales and production who make books happen.